ל"ט מלאכות

Second Grade Presentation

Sefer Dedications

In honor of Rabbi Posnick
לז"נ הרב יהודה אלחנן דיסקינד
Rabbi and Mrs. Boruch Ber Bender

•

לז"נ יוסף יהושע בן ישראל
Rabbi and Mrs. Yeshaya Yosef Kraus

•

In honor of Rabbi Nachumson
and our son Meir
Meir-we are so proud of you!
Keep up the good work
Mr. and Mrs. Menachem Frischman

•

In Honor of the 2nd Grade of
Yeshiva Darchei Torah
May the boys go מחיל אל חיל
Mr. and Mrs. Menachem Jacobowitz

•

In honor of their grandson
Kalman Daniel Chaitovsky
and his classmates
Meryl and Aaron Chaitovsky

•

לז"נ רחל בת שלמה
Mr. and Mrs. Yoily Edelstein

•

In honor of Nosson Lopiansky
Rabbi and Mrs. Yaakov Lopiansky

•

In honor of our grandson
Alex Nelkenbaum
And in memory of his great
grandparents
לז"נ משה בן בן ציון
לז"נ יהודית לביאה בת שמעון
Harry & Brigitte Schlachter

•

In honor of all the amazing
Rabbeim of Yeshiva
Darchei Torah
לז"נ
אלחנן אריה ליב בן יצחק
עמרם בן דוד שלמה
Rabbi and Mrs. Benzion Schwadel

•

In honor of our children
Rabbi and Mrs. Yehudah Zachter

Harav Shmuel P. Traube

Rabbi of the Beis Pinchas *beis medrash* of Belz, member of Harav Moshe Klein's *beis din*

Sokolov 38, Bnei Brak / tel: (03) 619-3319

I wish to affirm that I have examined the wonderful *Hashomrim Hatze'irim* about the halachos of the 39 *melachos* forbidden on Shabbos, after it was planned and edited by my capable son-in-law, Harav Moshe Vind, *shlit"a*, of Yerushalayim. I verified that all the halachos it contains are correct and that they follow the decisions of the great *Poskim* of the past and the present. One can confidently rely on the halachos presented here for practical use.

I must add that this wonderful *sefer*, fully illustrated as it is, is a splendid educational tool to teach the principles of Shabbos to young children. It is written in clear language and using a style that will hold the child's interest. I have no doubt that this is a *sefer* that children will pick up on their own to read and enjoy, gaining playful pleasure and Torah knowledge in one blow.

I extend my prayer that my son-in-law and his wife will continue to make practical halachos available to young children in such clear and easy language, and that they will be privileged to enjoy much satisfaction from their own children, with health and good spirits, wealth and honor, Amen.

With great esteem,
Shmuel P. Traube

Harav Shammai Kehas Hakohen Gross, shlit"a

I heartily recommend *Hashomrim Hatze'irim*, which teaches youngsters the complicated halachos of Shabbos in a practical system, so that they know what they may do and what they may not. The *sefer* is formatted in an attractive style that draws the reader and holds his attention. Each halachah is described and illustrated clearly. The entire *sefer* was carefully examined and edited by Harav Moshe Vind, *shlit"a*, to ensure that the halachos are taught correctly. Afterward, I went over all the material to make sure that there are no mistakes or misconceptions.

I am confident that everyone who brings this *sefer* into his home will reap the benefit of teaching these halachos to his young children. It will instill *yiras Shamayim* in their hearts, and they will then pay attention to what they are doing and ask their parents and teachers how to keep the halachah.

With the Torah's blessings,
Shammai Kehas Gross Hakohen

Harav Yisrael Gans

Panim Me'irot St. 2

Kiryat Mattersdorf, Yerushalayim

Adar II, 5774/2014

I was recently shown the book *Hashomrim Hatze'irim*, which was compiled by Harav Moshe Vind, *shlit"a*. I found it to be quite useful, presenting all the *melachos* of Shabbos through clear illustrations, giving young readers a basic understand of the halachic concepts.

I wish to give my hearty blessing to the esteemed author so that he can continue his wonderful work to bring our spiritual treasures to our people.

Yisrael Gans

הרב שמואל פ. טרויבע

רב ביהמ״ד בעלזא 'בית פינחס'

ומו״ץ בבית הוראה של הגרמ״ש קליין

רח' סוקולוב 38 ב״ב / טל': 6193319-03

בס״ד   יום ב' לס' 'וישמרו בנ״י את השבת'

הריני לאשר כי עברתי על כל הספר הנפלא 'השומרים הצעירים' בהלכות ל״ט מלאכות שבת, שנערך ונסדר מעשה אמן ע״י חתני המו״מ בת״ו והוראה הרה״ג ר' משה וינד שליט״א מעיה״ק ירושלים תובב״א, וראיתי כי כל ההלכות בו נכונות עפ״י הוראותיהם של גדולי הפוסקים זצוק״ל ויבלחט״א שמפיהם אנו חיים ומבארם אנו שותים, ובהחלט שניתן לסמוך 'למעשה' על כל המובא בספר זה.

מוכרחני לציין, כי הספר הנפלא – המלווה באיורים וציורים – הוא כלי נפלא להנחיל את מורשת הלכות שבת לצעירי הצאן, בשפה ברורה ומוחשית, מובנת ומרתקת, ומבלי ספק שמדובר בדבר גדול עבור תשב״ר שיעיינו ויקראו בו, ויוכלו לברך 'ברכת הנהנין' ו'ברכת התורה' בחדא מחתא.

ואני תפילה, שיזכה חתני הנ״ל וזוג' שתחי' להמשיך להפיץ דבר ה' זו הלכה בקרב צעירי הצאן בשפה מובנת וקלה, ויזכו לרוב נחת דקדושה מיוצ״ח נ״י, מתוך בריות גופא ונהורא מעליא, אושר ועושר וכבוד, וכט״ס בגו״ר. אכי״ר.

המברך בהערכה רבה

שמוא' פ. טרויבע

[חתימה]

הסכמת הרה״ג ר' שמאי קהת הכהן גרוס שליט״א

הנני בזה להמליץ על הספר הנפלא 'השומרים הצעירים', המלמד דעת את צעירי הצאן בהלכות שבת החמורות, שידעו את המעשה אשר יעשון וממה ימנעו.

והנה הספר נערך בצורה מיוחדת ומושכת את לב הקורא, וטוב מראה עיניים, שהכל מתבאר בהמחשה ובבהירות.

וביותר שהספר נערך אחרי יגיעה והתעמקות בהלכות אלו ע״י **הרה״ג ר' משה וינד שליט״א**, ואח״כ עברתי על הספר כולו להגיהו, שיהיה ראוי לנהוג על פיו הלכה למעשה ללא מכשול.

ובטוח אני שכל המביאו אל ביתו, יראה תועלת בהעברת הלכות אלו גם לילדים הצעירים, ויחדיר בקרבם את היראה הטהורה, שידעו להתבונן במעשיהם ולברר את ההלכות אצל הוריהם ומוריהם.

הרב
שמאי קהת גרוס
מו״ץ דקהל מחזיקי חרת באי״ה
דברי חיים 7
קרית בעלזא
ירושלים

הרב ישראל גנס

רח' פנים מאירות 2
קרית מטרסדורף, ירושלים 94423

בס״ד ....אדר. ב.. תשע..ה.

הובא לפני הספר "השומרים הצעירים" שנתחבר ע״י אברך ת״ח, הרה״ג ר' מ.וינד שליט״א.

והנה יש תועלת גדולה בו באשר הוא מקיף את לימוד מלאכות שבת הקשות בצורה מוחשית, ומקנה לצעירים ידיעה בהלכות הנ״ל.

ולא נצרכה אלא לברכה, שיזכה המחבר שליט״א להוסיף תת תנובה לזיכוי הרבים.

[חתימה]

THE HALACHAH MASTERS
LET'S LEARN THE HALACHOS OF SHABBOS

Copyright © 2020 by Tfutza Publications
ISBN: 978-1-60091-797-4

Tfutza
Publications

Tfutza Publications
P.O.B. 50036
Beitar Illit 90500
Tel: 972-2-650-9400
info@tfutzapublications.com

First published in Hebrew as *Hashomrim Hatzeirim*

Translator: R. Cywiak
Torah Editor: Rav Moshe Mizrahi
Torah Editor of the Hebrew edition: Rav Moshe Vind
Illustrator: Mrs. G. Vind
Cover designer: T. Frankel
Typesetter: Hadassa Segal

Distributed by:
Israel Bookshop Publications
501 Prospect Street
Lakewood, NJ 08701
Tel: (732) 901-3009
Fax: (732) 901-4012
www.israelbookshoppublications.com
info@israelbookshoppublications.com

Distributed in Israel by:
Tfutza Publications
P.O.B. 50036
Beitar Illit 90500
Tel: 972-2-650-9400
info@tfutzapublications.com

Distributed in Europe by:
Lehmanns
Unit E Viking Industrial Park
Rolling Mill Road
Jarrow, Tyne & Wear NE32 3DP
44-191-430-0333

Distributed in Australia by:
Golds World of Judaica
3-13 William Street
Balaclava 3183
613-9527-8775

Distributed in S. Africa by:
Kollel Bookshop
Ivy Common
107 William Road, Norwood
Johannesburg 2192
27-11-728-1822

Printed in Israel

THE HALACHAH MASTERS

LET'S LEARN THE HALACHOS OF SHABBOS

"אָמַר לוֹ הַקָּדוֹשׁ בָּרוּךְ הוּא לְמֹשֶׁה: 'מַתָּנָה טוֹבָה יֵשׁ לִי בְּבֵית גְּנָזַי וְשַׁבָּת שְׁמָהּ, וַאֲנִי מְבַקֵּשׁ לִתְּנָהּ לְיִשְׂרָאֵל. לֵךְ וְהוֹדִיעֵם'".

(שבת י', ע"ב)

Written and illustrated by Mrs. G. Vind
Reviewed by Rabbi Moshe Vind

Preface

The Blessed Holy One said to Moshe: "I have a wonderful gift in My treasure trove, and it is called Shabbos. I want to give it to the people of Yisrael. Go and tell them." (Shabbos 10b)

It Is an Eternal Symbol

Shabbos symbolizes the bond between the Creator and His nation Yisrael. It is a special connection, like a secret code shared by two close friends and no one else. Likewise, Shabbos is meant only for the Jewish people; a non-Jew may not observe Shabbos. Shabbos is the inner chamber of Hashem's throne room; no one may enter unless the king extends his scepter and invites him. (based on the *Nesivos Shalom*)

The main element of this mitzvah is to refrain from performing *melachah*. Our Sages taught that there are 39 categories of *melachah* forbidden on Shabbos, those that were employed in the construction of the Mishkan. The mitzvah of refraining from *melachah* has deep meaning and significance. The *Sefer Chinuch*, explains, "Shabbos gives us freedom from our personal affairs. We concentrate on honoring this day so that we affirm our belief that Hashem created the world. That is the fundamental principle preceding all other religious concepts." We ought to learn how to make the best use of this wonderful gift.

The Importance of Studying Hilchos Shabbos

Everyone understands the importance of knowing the halachos of Shabbos. The *Mishnah Berurah* states: "It is almost impossible to observe Shabbos in every detail. The only practical solution is to study the halachos thoroughly and review them regularly. That way, you will readily know what is permissible and what is not. Without intense and constant study, you might wish with all your heart and soul to observe Shabbos and still not observe it properly."

With every move that someone makes on Shabbos he might be unwittingly performing one of the 39 *melachos*. You can say, "I know enough not to sow seeds, plow, tear down structures, or build." But you will eat and drink, and that exposes you to many of the *melachos*, such as cooking, sorting, kneading, and more.

The Makeup of This Book

Every Jewish home has many books about *hilchos Shabbos*. The book you are holding is unique, however. It enables even a six-year-old child to know how to avoid desecrating Shabbos. It graphically describes the *melachos* in a manner that goes directly into the child's heart and mind. The result will be a child who is fluent in the basics of *hilchos Shabbos*. The halachos are taught through a playful and interesting plot, and because it is a comic book everything is fully illustrated. The child will happily read the book for his own enjoyment, and this important information will automatically register in his memory.

Many long hours were invested in clarifying the halachos, organizing them, choosing what to include in the book, and figuring out how to present them in an attractive, captivating manner. Aware that different communities follow different opinions in halachah, we chose to present the most basic concepts of the *melachos*, which are appropriate for every Torah community. In cases of fundamental differences, the reader is told to ask his parents for specific instructions. In the footnotes, we pointed out many instances of a *machlokes* between the *Mechaber* and Rema.

We worked hard to provide the exact sources for the halachos. In any case where the halachah seemed unclear to us, we brought it to competent Rabbanim for clarification. The entire manuscript was critically examined by Harav Shammai Kehas Hakohen Gross, *shlit"a*, who made a number of corrections. We are most grateful for his contribution.

As we go to print, we wish to thank Hashem for bringing us to this day and ask Him to continue to protect us from stumbling. It is our wish to see that this *sefer* will spread Torah knowledge and *yiras Shamayim* among *Klal Yisrael*, especially the children.

Acknowledgements

First and foremost, I must mention my esteemed father, Harav Aharon Vind, *shlit"a*, who stood by my side throughout this project. Likewise, I must thank my father-in-law, Harav Shmuel Pinchas Traube, *shlit"a*, who serves as *dayan* for the Machazikei Hadas community and as Rav of the Beis Pinchas *beis medrash* in Bnei Brak. He oversaw the publication of this book as a serial column in *Marveh Latzamei* magazine.

Harav Asher Yeshayahu Zalfriend, *shlit"a*, *dayan* for the Machazikei Hadas community and Rav of the Or Shlomo *beis medrash* in Ashdod, and Harav Yehudah Gans, son of Rav Yisrael, *shlit"a*, carefully examined the entire *sefer* and made corrections wherever necessary.

Harav Yitzchak Traube painstakingly arranged the source material, presenting it in the orderly and attractive style.

The editorial staff of *Marveh Latzamei* magazine first presented the material of this *sefer* (the Hebrew edition) as a serial column. Tfutza Publications recognized the enormous potential of this *sefer* and expanded it, having it translated into English by the capable Mrs. R. Cywiak. Harav Moshe Mizrahi served as Torah editor for the English rendition.

Introduction

Meet Yossi and Betzalel.

Yossi is a boy like any other, but he discovered a mysterious treasure chest. Betzalel is a friendly boy who has jumped right out of the pages of a history book. He hands Yossi an antique key with which he is able to open the chest.

The Blessed Holy One gave us a wonderful gift from His treasure chest, called Shabbos. But in order to be able to use this gift properly, we need a key. Betzalel will open the chest for us and tell us what he remembers from his experiences in the Midbar when he watched the construction of the Mishkan.

More than just tell what happened, his main purpose is to teach. He teaches us about the 39 *avos melachos*, so that we can take good care of our wonderful gift.

The construction of the Mishkan involved a great number of activities. *Chazal* listed them and called them the 39 *avos melachos*. These *melachos* are divided into four groups:

There are 11 *melachos* involved in the making of the dyes that were used for dyeing the *yerios* that covered the Mishkan: *zorei'a, choreish, kotzeir, me'ameir, dosh, zoreh, boreir, tochein, merakeid, losh,* and *ofeh*.

There are 13 *melachos* involved in making the *yerios* themselves: *gogeiz, melabein, menapeitz, tzovei'a, toveh, meiseich, ha'oseh shtei battei nirin, oreig, potzei'a, kosheir, matir, tofeir,* and *korei'a*.

There are 7 *melachos* involved in making the leather covers of the Mishkan: *tzad, shocheit, mafshit, me'abeid, memacheik, mesarteit,* and *mechateich*.

There are 8 other *melachos* involved in making the Mishkan: *koseiv, mocheik, boneh, soseir, mechabeh, mav'ir, makkeh bepatish,* and *hamotzi meirshus lirshus*.

All these *melachos* are forbidden on Shabbos.

Together, Yossi and Betzalel explain what the *melachos* are and show us the functions of each one. Sometimes, they call upon Betzalel's grandfather to show everyone how a particular *melachah* was performed in constructing the Mishkan. The most important lesson, however, is that they teach us to ask, to clarify, and to listen to the instructions we receive about the halachah.

Take a peek at the next column – Yossi and Betzalel are waiting!

The Torah Source for 39 Avos Melachos

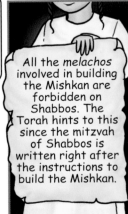

Basic Terms

Av Melachah and Toladah

Betzalel, is it true that you lived in tents in the desert?

Yes!

So come help me build a tent to play with!

But this is not like the tents we lived in...Our tents were sturdy and set in place. They were our homes!

It is forbidden on Shabbos to set up a tent like we lived in, since it ine is a *toladah* of the *melachah* of *boneh*, building. Mid'Rabbanan, it is even forbidden to set up a temporary tent.[2]

Doesn't *tolados* mean a child? How's that have to do with *melachah*?

An *av melachah* is work that was actually done in building the Mishkan. A *toladah* is work that resembles what was done in the Mishkan.[3] Just like a boy looks like his father, a *toladah* resembles an *av melachah*.

Issurim Mid'Rabbanan and Gezeiros of Chazal

Betzalel, you've taught me about *avos* and *tolados*, and you told me that the Torah forbids both!

That's right!

Well, we learned today in cheder that there are also things forbidden on Shabbos mid'Rabbanan.

Oy! I got so excited that I spilled the drink that you served me!

Well, now I can show you an example. You are not allowed to write with the liquid on the table. That is an *issur* mid'Rabbanan![4]

Why are you writing with your finger? Don't you have a quill?

We don't write with quills anymore! We use pens to write!

You reminded me of something else: Chazal made *gezeiros* so that people won't come close to doing a *melachah*.

For example: The pen is *muktzeh*, and we are not allowed to handle it on Shabbos,[5] because we might forget and write. It is a *kli shemelachto l'issur*.* That is a *gezeirah* of Chazal.[6]

Wait, we have *avos*, *tolados*, *issurim* mid'Rabbanan, *gezeiros* of Chazal, *zorei'a*, *choreish*, *kotzeir* — how will I remember?!

No need to do it all at once!

We'll learn a little each time!

---

*This is one reason for the prohibition of muktzeh, but there are other reasons.

Zorei'a
Sowing

What Is This Melachah, and How Was It Used in Building the Mishkan

Tell me, what are those seeds? Are they for dyes?

I don't know what dyes are. I'm sowing tomato seeds!

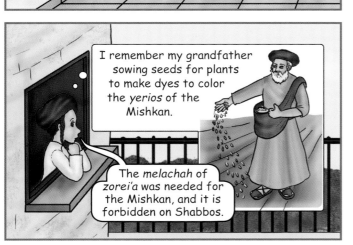

I remember my grandfather sowing seeds for plants to make dyes to color the *yerios* of the Mishkan.

The *melachah* of *zorei'a* was needed for the Mishkan, and it is forbidden on Shabbos.

OK, you're growing tomatoes, but why are you singing?

Someone told me that singing to a plant helps it grow.

It can't hurt!

I don't know if singing helps or not.

I only know that any action that helps a plant grow is forbidden on Shabbos.[7]

The Av Melachah of Sowing Seeds

What other seeds can I plant? Maybe apple seeds?

You plant saplings, not apple seeds, and you need more than a little pot!

So maybe a clementine tree?

What's a clementine?

I never tasted the flavor of clementine in the *mann*!

A clementine is a fruit produced by crossing an orange and a mandarin.

You mean they put pollen from one tree into the blossoms of the other tree.

But clementines also grow on trees. What kind of seeds can I sow?

Maybe I just won't become a gardener!

You can decide for yourself.

But if you become a gardener, you have to know all about the *av melachah* of *zorei'a*. We already talked about sowing seeds and planting trees. There is also grafting branches onto trees,[8] bending a branch down into the ground so it becomes a new tree, and pruning to make the tree grow better.[9]

Zorei'a

Choreish
Plowing

The Tolados of Zorei'a

What Is this Melachah, and How Was It Used in Building the Mishkan

*Some say that if you weed, removes stones, or water plants on Shabbos, you are guilty also of performing *tolados* of *choreish*, plowing.[13]

Av Melachah of Choreish

I thought that you only hoe and plow in your garden. Do you do this work out here, too?

I want to hide something valuable. I've read in books that many people hide treasures next to trees.

Don't look at what I am hiding!

I'm not looking. Just tell me: How long will you keep your treasure in the ground?

I got candy so I'm hiding it until for Shabbos!

And you plan to dig it up on Shabbos?

Uh huh...That's my plan!

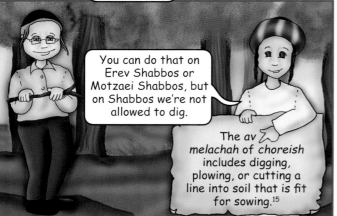

You can do that on Erev Shabbos or Motzaei Shabbos, but on Shabbos we're not allowed to dig.

The av melachah of choreish includes digging, plowing, or cutting a line into soil that is fit for sowing.[15]

Tolados of Choresh and Gezeiros of Chazal for Choreish

Why are you sweeping here?

But this sweeping never ends!

I want to play here and I don't want to get my pants dirty!

Okay, I'll just sweep enough to make the ground flat!

It's impossible to ever finish sweeping the ground You'll just have to accept the fact that your pants will get dirty.

I'll fill this hole with soil, and I'll flatten that little bump – and then we can start playing!

First we'll learn, and then we'll play:

Evening out the ground, like filling that hole or flattening that bump – is a toladah of choreish.[16]

To make sure we don't even smooth out the ground on Shabbos, Chazal made a gezeirah forbidding sweeping the ground unless it is covered with a floor.[17]

Do you know how to play marbles? I bet you had ancient marbles! 3,000-year-old marbles must be worth a fortune!

Will you play with me?

Sure, I'll play – but only with your marbles. I have none!

But you know – Chazal made a gezeirah forbidding playing on Shabbos with things like nuts or marbles on the bare ground.[18]

What Is this Melachah, and How Was It Used in Building the Mishkan

Av Melachah of Kotzeir and Its Tolados

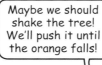

Kotzeir

Using Trees on Shabbos ל

You probably don't know how to climb trees!

That's right, but how do you know?

There are no trees in a desert, so you probably never practiced climbing!

It's also not such a good idea to climb trees. It's a tried-and-true way to fall down!

That's on weekdays, but on Shabbos we're not allowed to climb trees at all. That's a *gezeirah* of Chazal.[22]

Maybe we can swing from the tree? We'll make a swing with rope and a board!

Let's make sure to hang it on a strong branch! I don't want to fall!

Where did you get the board and the rope?

I have a hiding place in the tree. I put things there so no one will take them!

Putting things on a tree or taking things off a tree are ways of using the tree.

When we swing on a board hanging from the tree, we are using an item that is hanging on the tree.

Chazal made a *gezeirah* forbidding the use of a tree[23] or an object hanging from it[24] to make sure we don't break a branch off the tree.

ל Gezeiros of Chazal for Kotzeir

Why did you turn that way? I want you to turn this way! I want to get to the fruit.

He's not listening to me! I have to teach him like other riders do – with a stick!

Great! Now he's going towards these beautiful fruits so I can smell them!

Was I dreaming – or did that really happen?

I was riding a donkey and I wanted to reach the fruits to smell them!

Of course it was a dream. It's Shabbos today! All the things you did in your dream are forbidden on Shabbos!

A *gezeirah* of *Chazal* forbids riding or using animals on Shabbos,[25] since someone might break a stick off a tree to whip it.[26]

It is also forbidden to smell fruits that are connected to the ground because someone might pick one to eat it.[27]

Me'ameir
Gathering

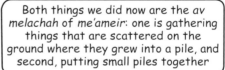

*Washing fruits into a solid mass or stringing them together is forbidden at home also.[30]

Rabbinical Prohibitions of Me'ameir

What Is this Melachah, and How Was It Used in Building the Mishkan

My uncle asked if we could help him collect the eggs in his coop!

Look at this chicken! She's guarding her eggs as if they were made of gold!

Yossi, You know what? I've been here for a long time. Why don't you come visit me in the desert!

Really? You want to take me there?

Oy! Two eggs broke! It's a good thing they are not gold...

So maybe we should help your uncle in some other way, like...

Wow! We're here already??

This is my grandfather! He is threshing his dye plants. How I've missed him!

Yes, yesterday a delivery of apples arrived. They were left in the yard and got scattered all around.

Let's collect them to one place!

By the way, what is threshing?

Shalom, young man! I understand that you are Betzalel's friend and you asked the meaning of the melachah of dosh.

Dosh means loosening the wanted kernel from its peel or shell.

We'll have to hurry, because it's almost Shabbos and we need to get ready.

We have to prepare for Shabbos,

And stop all things that are forbidden on Shabbos.

Rabbinical prohibitions:
> There are things that do not grow from the ground but still may not be collected such as eggs in a coop, since it is similar to me'ameir.[31]
> Things that grow from the ground and became scattered at home must not be collected even where they did not grow,[32] because it looks like weekday work.*

In order to loosen the kernels from their shells in the sheaves, we thresh them with a special tool.

Our work for building the Mishkan is to thresh the dyes.

Threshing grain with a tool is the av melachah of dosh,[35] and it is forbidden on Shabbos.

*Unless one gathers just a few to eat[33] or that fell in one place.[34]

Making fruit juice is forbidden on Shabbos; it is the *melachah* of *dosh*, because we separate drink from solid fruit. Juicing olives and grapes, which everyone in the world does, is forbidden by the Torah.[36] Fruits less commonly Juiced are forbidden *mid'Rabbanan*.[37]

Tolados of *dosh* are: Separating things that grew in the ground from parts that no one can eat, a job usually done in the field. Therefore, we may not remove beans from the pods by hand.[38] We may not milk cows on Shabbos, removing milk from the animal.[39]

Gezeiros: Juice That Seeps From Fruit, Crushing Snow or Ice

I am thirsty! You had a drink with you when we left for the Shabbos davening in shul. Is there any left?

I didn't bring it! I figured that we wouldn't need to drink on a cold day like this.

Hold on! I brought an orange to eat, but it got mashed and all the juice came out. Would you like to drink the juice?

We are allowed to drink the juice of an orange if it seeped out by itself on Shabbos, but there's not much here!

Maybe you could squeeze some snow into water?

We're not allowed to do that on Shabbos!

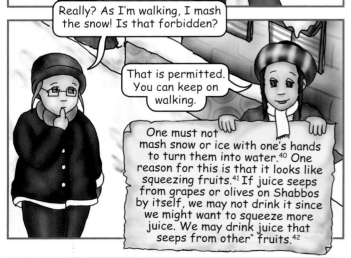

Really? As I'm walking, I mash the snow! Is that forbidden?

That is permitted. You can keep on walking.

One must not mash snow or ice with one's hands to turn them into water.[40] One reason for this is that it looks like squeezing fruits.[41] If juice seeps from grapes or olives on Shabbos by itself, we may not drink it since we might want to squeeze more juice. We may drink juice that seeps from other* fruits.[42]

*The same applies to strawberries, and pomegranates, or other fruits that are commonly squeezed for juice, even if they were purchased for that purpose.

What Is this Melachah, and How Was It Used in Building the Mishkan

What are you up to?

Yesterday you told me how your grandfather winnowed his dye plants by using a tool to throw them in the air. The wind blew away the straw and the heavier kernels fell straight down.

Since the year began, I've been filling my pencil case with pencil shavings, and now it's a mess of pencils, pens, and shavings. I'm trying to blow away the shavings by winnowing.

That's an original idea. Very original.

So let's try to define your original idea:

The melachah of zoreh is separating the unneeded chaff from the seeds using the wind.[43]

The av melachah is separating unneeded chaff using a tool, but the av melachah applies only to foods.

Using the wind to separate unneeded parts from things that are not food, like your crayons and pencils*, is forbidden mid'Rabbanan.[44]

*This example is not so relevant, because it is forbidden anyway because of muktzeh.

Tolados of Zoreh

It looked like you were playing jacks; I see now that this is a game of 100 peanuts.

You've had some very original ideas for games recently!

I don't like peanut shells, and I'm too lazy to peel them one at a time.

I'm trying to throw them in the air to winnow them, so that the peels will blow away!

But the peels aren't coming off at all! They won't come loose from the peanuts!

Maybe try blowing on them? Then the peels will come off easily!

You blew so hard that my scroll opened up.

Let's see what it says!

Throwing foods to the wind by hand for winnowing, or blowing away unwanted parts with your breath, is forbidden on Shabbos.[45] These are tolados of zoreh.

What Is this Melachah, and How Was It Used in Building the Mishkan

Too bad I was lazy yesterday and I didn't throw away the nut shells! Now they're all mixed up with the almonds and walnuts!

Betzalel, maybe you can help me? Everything is all mixed together here!

I see that food and waste are mixed up here. We'll have to sort them!

Sorting – my grandfather had to sort the kernels of dye from the waste that was mixed into them.

You know what Yossi? The melachah of boreir, sorting, comes up very often on Shabbos, and that's why we have to learn the details of the halachos carefully!

First, we'll define the melachah: separating unwanted stuff from what you want.[46]

Boreir

| Condition #1 for Sorting: Take The Good From The Bad | Condition #2 for Sorting: Do It With Bare Hands |

This strawberry is rotten.

These two are really mushy...

You've become very choosy lately. You keep on picking and choosing!

I don't want my noodles with mushroom sauce!

I want my noodles without mushroom sauce!

I'm helping my mother make a Shabbos dessert.

Is that why you are taking out the bad ones – the strawberries you don't want?

You're going to pick the noodles one at a time from the mushrooms?

I thought about doing it with my fingers, but maybe a sieve would be better!

If we want to sort things on Shabbos, we have to meet three conditions.

Today I'll teach you the first one.

But meanwhile I'm going to sort these strawberries, okay?

Good, pour the noodles into this sieve. Maybe the job will be easier with this tool!

No good! The holes are too small!

Sure!

Now I'm going to separate one for you – *ochel*, the one we want, from *pesoles*, that we don't.

Condition #1: Take *ochel*, what you want to eat from the *pesoles*, the unwanted:[47] Pick good ones from the rotten ones.

Clean it well and you can enjoy!

I think that I'd better just cook more noodles without mushrooms!

And I'll teach you another rule:

Another condition to be allowed to sort things on Shabbos: Do it by hand, and not with a tool.[48]

Boreir

Condition #3 for Sorting: For Immediate Use [49]

What Are Ochel and Pesoles

Separating From a Mixture of Two Foods

Sorting Other Items

I really love to help! I also want to put each cake away in the right place!

I'll put the rugelach in their box, the chocolate cake in another box, and the jelly cookies in their container.

Let's show how organized we can be! We'll prepare now our clothes for tomorrow!

Stop! What you're doing is forbidden. It's *boreir!*

But I saw you sorting cakes. I learned from you that I can do it!

This is my shirt; here is your hat!

That's my robe, and here's your yarmulke!

These are my pants...

The cakes that I put away weren't mixed at all. There were slices of chocolate cake on one plate,

and the rugelach were on another plate, so I put each cake back in its box.

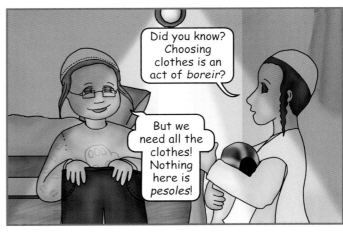

Did you know? Choosing clothes is an act of *boreir?*

But we need all the clothes! Nothing here is *pesoles!*

I see! My plate has several types of cakes mixed together. So I am not allowed to sort them and put each one in its place.

The *issur* of *boreir* applies to different foods mixed together. When each food is clearly separate from the others, there is no *issur* of *boreir*.[51]

We are choosing one thing from others when we don't plan to use it right now!

Choosing from mixed items to use them at a later time is included in the *melachah* of *boreir*, and it is forbidden on Shabbos.[52]

Peeling Fruits and Vegetables

 What Is this Melachah, and How Was It Used in Building the Mishkan

Tochein

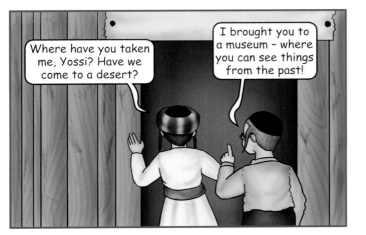

27

Tochein

Grinding Things That Grow From the Ground and Things That Do Not

Today is Tuesday, right?

Today is Tuesday, yes!

And you're already preparing eggs for Shabbos?

Shammai the Tanna did things for Shabbos every day of the week, as you know!

But I think it's not a good idea. Eggs must be fresh to taste good!

I'll help you prepare them on Shabbos!

Are we allowed to mash eggs or chop them up on Shabbos?

Tochein applies to plants only. We can mash eggs on Shabbos because they do not grow in the ground,[58] and because we can eat them without mashing them.

Even so, we must not chop eggs with a tool made specially for that purpose, like a grater.[59]

Merakeid — Sifting

What Is this Melachah, and How Was It Used in Building the Mishkan

This is my first cake. I hope it comes out good!

Why are you making the flour jump like that?

Jump? That's how we sift it!

Would you like to do it also?

That's interesting!

In building the Mishkan, the *melachah* of *merakeid* was done to sift the crushed dye bits!

Oh, you have been sifting for thousands of years! So come and help me!

Sure!

The *av melachah* of *merakeid* is to use a sifter to separate flour from bits that we don't want.[60]

Losh
Kneading

What Is this Melachah, and How Was It Used in Building the Mishkan

What Is a Thick Batter? What's the Halachah?

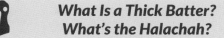

29

Belilah Rakah – A Thin Batter

Winter is coming and it's getting chilly. How about some hot cereal?

You once told me that hot cereal is baby food, didn't you?

Yes, but there are kinds of hot cereal that we would like!

You put farina or oats into a pot, and add milk.

You can add salt or sugar if you want.

Cook it for a few minutes – and there you are – hot cereal!

I don't think I will like this cereal.

But it's a great example of a belilah rakah – a thin batter.

It is forbidden mid'Rabbanan to mix a thin batter[63] – a mixture that you can pour from one container to another. This is permissible only under certain circumstances.[64]

This will be explained in the next panel.

When Can a Thin Batter be Made on Shabbos

To make a thin batter on Shabbos you have to use a shinui, a different way than you usually do it:

The first shinui: change the order you put the ingredients in the bowl.

If, during the week, we first put in the farina and then the milk, then on Shabbos we first put in the milk and then the farina.

Weekday   Shabbos

And if we usually pour the milk in first, then on Shabbos we will first put in the farina.[65]

Some say that we need to make a second shinui: the way we stir.

Usually, we stir in a circular motion.

On Shabbos, we stir with a criss-cross motion.

First move the spoon across the bowl from right to left,

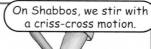

And then across from front to back. Then repeat the steps.[66]

There are other ways to stir with a shinui: shaking the bowl or mixing with your hand.[67]

Kneading a thick batter on Shabbos is forbidden even if done with a shinui.

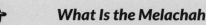

It's interesting that, one day you make real cakes, and the next day you make mud cakes!

I'm playing with my brother!

Why are you cooking potatoes?

So I can eat them!

But where is he?

I wasn't paying attention. Where is he?

What makes the potatoes get cooked?

What's the question? I am cooking the potatoes so I can eat them!

I went to get more water to mix with the sand, so that the cakes would look like real!

You mean you make them ready to eat with the heat of the fire.

What's with you today? Why so many questions and answers?

It's just potatoes!

Now we have cake for Shabbos!

These cakes really prepare us for Shabbos, because they remind us of the *halachah*:

Regarding things like thick sand, simply adding water is considered *losh* even without stirring it[68]

That's true, but this brings us to our next *melachah*: *bishul*, cooking.

The definition of *bishul* is making something ready for use with the heat of a fire.[69]

We have lots to learn! Let's get going!

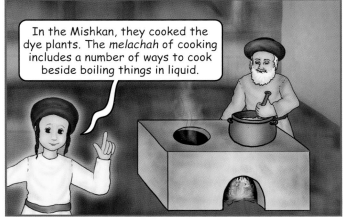

In the Mishkan, they cooked the dye plants. The *melachah* of cooking includes a number of ways to cook beside boiling things in liquid.

Yossi, tell me how to prepare this egg so I can eat it.

That's simple!

Put a pan or pot on the stove and turn on the fire.

For example, we bake food in an oven.

And you can make a hard-boiled egg, a scrambled egg, or however you would like it!

But any of those choices means cooking with fire!

And we fry food in a bit of oil.

According to most *poskim*, deep frying in oil is the same as cooking in liquid.[70]

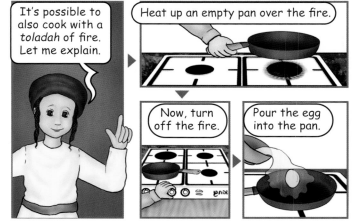

It's possible to also cook with a *toladah* of fire. Let me explain.

Heat up an empty pan over the fire.

Now, turn off the fire.

Pour the egg into the pan.

We can broil food over a fire.

Like the livers my mother broiled yesterday!

All these types of *bishul* are forbidden on Shabbos.[71]

The egg is ready!

The pan was heated by the fire but the egg was cooked by the heated frying pan, not by the fire itself. That is called *toledes eish*.

Cooking with fire or with *toledes eish* is forbidden on Shabbos.[72]

There is no room in the kitchen for the eggs so I put them out on the porch for now.

I'm afraid they will get spoiled! You should move them into the shade.

What are you writing?

I'm trying to summarize.

One must not cook with fire, or in something heated by a fire.

Wait!

I wasn't careful enough! One egg fell and broke!

I'll clean it up soon!

What about a pot full of water that was heated over the fire?

In the melachah of bishul there are different levels of heat. Water has to reach a certain level and then it can cook things.

I completely forgot about cleaning the mess!

Look! It's so hot today that the egg got cooked!

Of course. The sun's heat can cook as well!

Something that was heated by the sun can also cook things.

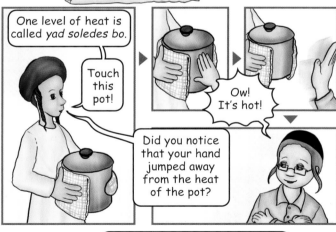

One level of heat is called yad soledes bo.

Touch this pot!

Ow! It's hot!

Did you notice that your hand jumped away from the heat of the pot?

If you pour an egg on a pan that had been in the sun's heat for a while, it will get cooked.

We may cook with the sun's heat on Shabbos, but not with toledes chamah, because people might mistakenly cook with toledes eish.[73]

That is called yad soledes bo![74] There is another level called yad nichveis bo.[75]

But I won't ask you to touch it since your hand might really get burned!

Later on we will learn the halachah that applies to each of these levels of heat.

Kli rishon, kli sheini, kli shlishi...

Why are you counting pots?

Ow! This pot is boiling hot!

But there is no fire under it!

The fire was on until 15 minutes ago.

I'm not counting pots; I'm trying to teach about different containers regarding Shabbos.

A pot standing on the fire is called a *kli rishon*.

Even after it is taken off the fire, it is still a *kli rishon*.[76]

But the pot is still hot.

This pot is called a *kli rishon* right?

When we pour the cooked food from the pot into a bowl, the bowl is called a *kli sheini*.

And if we transfer the food from the *kli sheini* into another container, that is a *kli shlishi*.

Indeed, and as long as it is as hot as *yad soledes bo*, we must not put anything uncooked into it on Shabbos – even if the fire is not on.

So when are we allowed to add raw food to hot cooked food?

It depends how hot it is, what type of *kli it is*, and what type of food it is.

I see you have another pot here!

That's right, but look at that! I put it on the fire, and it's not hot at all!

Be patient! It takes time to warm up!

But even while the pot is not yet hot we are not allowed to put food into a pot on the fire, even if the food was already cooked.[77]

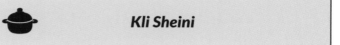

Careful!

Oy!

All the hot water spilled!

Is this pot a *kli rishon* or a *kli sheini*?

A *kli sheini*: I poured the soup into it from another pot.

Did you notice the color of the chicken? The surface suddenly looks a bit cooked!

Of course! Water poured from a *kli rishon* cooks the surface layer (*k'dei kelipah*) of the food it lands on.[78]

Ow! The soup is still really hot! My hand pulls back from it!

Am I allowed to put an uncooked potato into such a hot *kli sheini*?

What did we learn in the Gemara?

And therefore –

It is forbidden on Shabbos to pour from a *kli rishon* that is *yad soledes bo* onto raw food[79] like potatoes or chicken.

You keep talking about solid foods. What about liquids?

That a *kli sheini* does not cook!

It can only cook *kalei habishul*.

Is a potato one of those foods?

Those are things that cook also at lower temperatures.[82]

Nowadays, we don't know which foods are considered *kalei habishul*, and so in practice we cannot put any raw food into a *kli sheini* that is *yad soledes bo*.[83]

Am I allowed to pour from a *kli rishon* that is *yad soledes bo* into a cup of cold water?

If you add just a little hot water, and the water that is in the cup will not become *yad soledes bo* – it is permitted.[80]

But if you add lots of hot water so that the water in the cup becomes *yad soledes bo* – that is not allowed.[81]

Are there foods that are definitely not *kalei habishul*?

Yes! Water and oil are not *kalei habishul*, and they can be added to a *klei sheini*, even if it is *yad soledes bo*.[84]

Kli Shlishi

I'm c-c-old! Maybe tea will warm me up.

The cup of hot water is a *kli sheini*, right?

Yes, and I'm pouring it into a *kli shlishi* right now, because I like drinking from this cup.

Too bad I didn't put the tea bag into the *kli sheini*!

Can a *kli shlishi* cook things?

It depends what!

A *kli shlishi* can cook things that are definitely *kalei bishul*, that cook with very little heat. One example is salted fish.[85]

As for making tea, we are not allowed to prepare tea on Shabbos even in a *kli shlishi*, because it also cooks easily.[86]

And now, drink up!

Davar Goosh – A Solid

Potato kugel, fresh from the oven!

My mother made a few individual portions for us to eat before Shabbos!

Do you want a slice of salami* with it?

Yes, but don't put it on the kugel. I prefer my salami cold.

Right. The kugel is in a *kli rishon*, and it can heat up the salami.*

Maybe if we put the kugel in another plate, a *kli sheini*, so it won't be able to cook the salami or warm it up.

Kugel is a solid food.

A solid food can cook even if it is in a *kli sheini*, a *kli shlishi*, or more.[87] It does not cool down as soon as it is placed in another dish.

As long as the kugel is as hot as *yad soledes bo*, it can still cook something else.

So, will two separate plates be good for you?

*Smoked salami is not considered *mevushal* – cooked.

36

Bishul Achar Bishul – Cooking a Second Time

Hey! This hot pot is a *kli rishon* that I just took off the fire, isn't it?

That's right!

So how can you put a piece of chicken into it? You said that we are not allowed to put food into a *kli rishon*!

We must not put any raw food into a *kli rishon*, but this piece of chicken was already cooked!

But you're cooking it again!

Ein bishul achar bishul. It is not considered cooking if the food* has already been completely cooked.[88]

The chicken is a solid food. What about a liquid food like soup?

There are varying opinions regarding whether this concept applies to liquid foods like soup.[89]

Ask your father what your *minhag* is.

And when I get back to the Midbar I'll find out for myself![90]

---

*Some *poskim* are *machmir* as long as the bones have not yet been fully cooked.

Bishul Achar Afiyah – Cooking Something That Was Baked

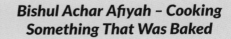

Why are you putting bourekas into the sauce?

Usually, we pour the sauce over the bourekas, right?

I couldn't find a ladle or a spoon.

Now I can take out the bourekas with a fork also!

The sauce is in a *kli rishon*, isn't it?

Yes, but it's not Shabbos today.

Besides, you told me there's no *bishul* after *bishul*!

The bourekas are already cooked!

The bourekas are only baked. And there is a problem with cooking it with hot liquid

There are varying opinions about doing it in a kli sheini.*

In a *kli shlishi* it is definitely permitted.

One must not put a baked item into a *kli rishon* if it is *yad soledes bo* on Shabbos.[91]

Is that why you told me this today? This way, by Shabbos I can find out how we do it.

---

*For the different opinions, please see footnote [92].

Shehiyah – Why Is There a Problem

When Shehiyah Is Permitted on a Kirah (Gerufah or Ketumah)

It's Shabbos!

Of course. What do you mean to tell me?

So now teach me when it is permissible to put a pot back on the fire after taking it off.

I'll teach you and you'll repeat the following conditions:

You said that on Shabbos it is forbidden to put a pot on the fire or a warming tray.

You stressed that it is forbidden even if the food is fully cooked.

And you explained that if we put cooked food on a fire it still looks like we are cooking on Shabbos!

Is the fire gerufah or ketumah?

Of course! It's a warming tray. No fire can be seen!

Is the food completely cooked?

Yes!

If only you had come into the kitchen a minute earlier!

You would have seen me take this pot off the warming tray and keep holding it in my hand.

And is it still hot?

Yes! I have to hold it with this towel...

Did you let go of the pot?

No! Not even for a second!

Now I'm allowed to put it back in its place!

Chazal allowed us to put a pot back onto the fire under certain conditions.[96]

When you picked up the pot, did you plan to put it back?

Sure!

If all those things are true, then you may put the pot back on the warming tray.[97]

Hatmanah – What Is the Problem?

Hey, what happened?

A blackout!

Oy! The warming tray is also off!

What are we going to do? All the food is getting cold!

Do you know what we did to keep food warm? We wrapped it in something that kept the warmth inside!

On weekdays, My grandmother also used to cover her pot with a big towel on all sides to keep it hot!

But we are not allowed to do that on Shabbos!

We always wrapped up the food on Erev Shabbos.

Chazal said that if someone wraps up his food on Shabbos, he might decide that the food is not hot enough, and then he will reheat it on Shabbos.[98] So they made a gezeirah that hatmanah on Shabbos is forbidden except in special cases.

Hatmanah - Wrapping With Material That Does Not Add Heat

You taught me about the issur of hatmanah.

But I still don't understand: what does a blanket or towel do? Does it heat the food?

There are two types of hatmanah:

One is to wrap it with a davar hamosif hevel, something that can make food hotter.

Salt and sand are things that can do that.

And then there is hatmanah using material that cannot make food hotter.

When we wrap a pot in a towel, the towel does not make the pot any hotter.

I see! It just keeps the heat already there longer!

You are allowed to wrap food on Erev Shabbos with material that does not make it hotter.[99]

So is this allowed on Shabbos also?

Are we allowed to do wrap food with material that adds heat?

When? On Shabbos?

On Erev Shabbos?

Try to be patient, Yossi? You'll get all the answers!

I waited patiently! Now can you teach me about *hatmanah*?

Yes! You deserve it!

You explained *hatmanah* with material that does not add heat.

Last time, we said that if a pot is wrapped in a towel, it just keeps the heat of the pot from escaping.

What if the pot is not hot enough and I want to wrap it in material that makes it hotter?

You also told me that on Erev Shabbos we are allowed to do *hatmanah* with something that does not add heat, and just holds the heat in, like a towel.

But you didn't answer me about Shabbos!

There are cases when it is permitted to do *hatmanah* on Shabbos to preserve heat, but not to make it hotter:

We used to put pots in the *kirah*. The ashes left inside still were hot enough to make the food hotter.

Can you give me an example of material that adds heat?

You can wrap cold food.[100]

Or a hot pot of fully cooked food that is already covered with one towel.[101]

Sure! If you wrap up a pot in a towel and put it on a warming tray, it adds heat.

However!

It is never permissible to do *hatmanah* with material that adds heat. Not even if you do it before Shabbos![104]

You can transfer the contents of the pot to another container, and then do *hatmanah*,[102] because the *gezeirah* of *hatmanah* applies only to the pot in which the food was cooked.

And you can wrap food in other food – this is not normal *hatmanah*.[103]

Some Poskim permitted *hatmanah* in material that adds heat, but only in special cases.

It's a good thing you are teaching me halachic concepts. This way I know that I have to ask which Poskim we follow!

Winding up the First Group of Melachos, Applying to Dye Plants

What Is this Melachah, and How Was It Used in Building the Mishkan

This is it? Are you going back to the desert?

What made you think that?

You're packing all your things, and the pictures that you brought.

You packed up all the pictures of the melachos involved in making the dyes, but you forgot to pack this one!

I didn't forget. I took it out from the new package.

Have you finished teaching me all the melachos?

How about counting with me how many we've learned?

Zorei'a, choreish, kotzeir, me'ameir, dosh, zoreh, boreir, tochein, merakeid, losh and bishul!

Do you see how my grandfather is shearing the wool?

Only eleven melachos! And there are 39!

So you can't go back to the desert yet!

I'm not going back!

I'm packing up the pictures that taught you about the melachos that were involved in preparing the dye plants.

In the Mishkan, they needed wool for the yerios and for the bigdei kehunah.

When you shear wool, you detach it from where it grew.

These plants were used to dye the skins and the woven material from which they made the yerios to cover the Mishkan.

Now I'm taking out a new package of pictures for the next set of melachos:

Melachos that were done in order to make woven material.

When we cut hair, a piece of skin or nails – we detach it from where it grew!

Detaching something from where it grew on a human body or an animal is included in the melachah of gozeiz.[105]

Gozeiz

Shearing Wool of an Animal

This lamb has so much wool!

We'll never finish shearing it!

I'll lend you a hand!

But we don't have another pair of scissors!

Can we pluck the wool out by hand?

We could, but it would hurt the lamb!

We are not allowed to hurt her!

Is plucking wool by hand included in the melachah of gozeiz?

The av melachah of gozeiz is shearing the wool or hair with a tool.

It is forbidden by the Torah to pluck the hair of a dead animal by hand on Shabbos.

Plucking the hair of a living animal is forbidden mid'Rabbanan; it is not the normal way to shear an animal[106] since it hurts.

Cutting Hair and Nails

Why is your finger in your mouth?

I'm a bit nervous, and so I started biting my nails.

That habit could give you problems! It might lead to chilul Shabbos!

Biting nails is forbidden mid'Rabbanan; it is forbidden by the Torah to cut them with a tool like scissors.[107]

You stopped playing with your nails, so now you play with your peyos??

I'm not playing with my peyos. I'm just combing them!

Oops! A few hairs came out!

Pulling out your hair on Shabbos is included in the melachah of gozeiz.[108]

That is why we cannot use a comb on our hair on Shabbos. We will pull hairs out for sure, and we will be guilty of the melachah of gozeiz.[109]

Melabein
Laundering

What Is this Melachah, and How Was It Used in Building the Mishkan

Washing Clothes in Water

Do you do anything today the same way we did it in the Midbar? Maybe the way you launder clothes?

You can't go out to the Chevras Tehillim that way!

What's the matter?

Oy! When did I get so dirty?

Not at all!

We have a washing machine that does a great job!

I'm just scrubbing this stain that came when I was eating chocolate cake.

But it's not a problem. A bit of water, and it will be all clean!

Of course it's a problem. We are not allowed to wash a garment with water on Shabbos![110]

You had to scrub every stain and every spot of dirt, didn't you?

Indeed. Melabein was part of the yerios process – they whitened the wool shorn from the sheep with water.

So we'll have to say Tehillim at home. I don't have anything else to wear!

Why are you cleaning that stain off the table?

Sheep don't keep clean – and neither does the wool.

And that is the next melachah we are going to learn about: melabein, laundering.

The wool could only be used for the yerios after it was whitened.

So that we can put our sifrei Tehillim down!

Laundering only applies to clothes, textiles, tablecloths – materials that absorb.

But you said it's forbidden to clean things on Shabbos!

It is okay to wash a hard object like a tabletop with water and to wipe away the dirt.[111]

44

Melabein

Removing Dirt from Clothing

Wringing Out Material

45

Melabein

Menapeitz
Combing

46

The Melachah in building the Mishkan

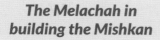

My brother scribbled on the wall with markers, pens, paint and whatever he could find!

So I decided to paint the wall white!

If I paint the walls white, is that the *melachah* of *melabein*, which means whitening?

You are painting walls, and that is part of the *melachah* of *tzovei'a*, dyeing.

After the wool was whitened and combed, it was dyed into different colors.

Caution! Wet Paint!

Show me the picture.

Do you see? Some of the wool was dyed purple, some was dyed *techeles*, and some was dyed red.

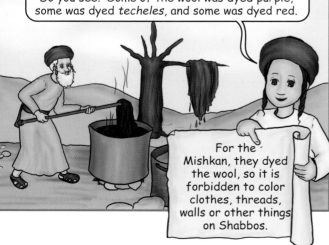

For the Mishkan, they dyed the wool, so it is forbidden to color clothes, threads, walls or other things on Shabbos.

Defining the Melachah

Is that tool you're holding used to dye shoes?

I'm not dyeing them. I polish shoes for the whole family every Shabbos!

Polishing shoes is included in *tzovei'a*.[117]

But I'm not changing their color at all!

I'm not coloring my sister's white shoes black, nor am I making blue shoes into brown ones!

But when I rub black polish on a black shoe, I make it more black than it was before!

The *melachah* of *tzovei'a* is to change something's color or to or strengthen the existing color.

Now, would you please polish my shoes?

I won't mind if you make them black!

My pleasure!

47

Coloring Foods

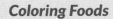

What Is This Melachah, and How Was It Used in Building the Mishkan

I've never seen such a giant calendar!

Can you help me turn the pages so that we can get to the year 2448?

2448 from Creation

Wow! We're in the ancient Midbar!

This is exactly where and when I wanted to get to – the year the Mishkan was built.

We're up to the *melachah* of *meisech*, setting up a loom and I have no way to explain it to you without bringing you here!

Now that we have thread, its time to weave it.

Woven material has threads stretching horizontally and others stretching vertically.

The first step in preparing material is to thread the *shesi*, the warp threads, on the loom. This is called *meiseich*.

I want to help you weave. It sounds interesting! Afterwards I'll be able to tell my friends all about it!

We've set up the warp threads. Next step!

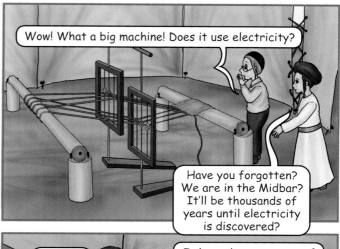

Wow! What a big machine! Does it use electricity?

Have you forgotten? We are in the Midbar? It'll be thousands of years until electricity is discovered?

This machine is called a loom – a weaving machine.

I showed you one way of weaving, by threading the warp onto a frame.

Another way is to use a loom.

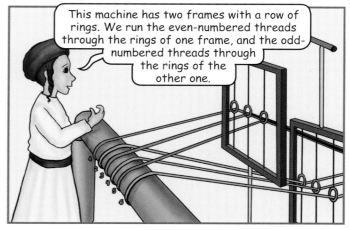

This machine has two frames with a row of rings. We run the even-numbered threads through the rings of one frame, and the odd-numbered threads through the rings of the other one.

These rings are called *batei nirin*, or heddles.

The *melachah* of preparing these rings, or of threading the *shesi* strings through them is called *oseh shtei batei nirin*, setting up the heddles.[122]

Then it will be easy to weave – we just run the weft threads through the warp threads.

Oreig — Weaving

What Is This Melachah, and How Was It Used in Building the Mishkan

I want to try weaving!

Okay, you see this? You run the weft threads between the warp threads.

First over the warp, and then under the warp.

That's so interesting! I never knew how material is made!

This is the *melachah* of weaving.

For the Mishkan, they wove the *yerios* that covered the Mishkan.

Will you let me take this piece of fabric home with me?

This fabric is in the middle of being woven, and I can't take it off the loom now! You'll have to make do with some leftover threads.

That's not very impressive, but I'll take them anyway to make my sister happy! She likes to make braids out of bunches of thread!

So go ahead. Gather the threads.

Just don't forget to tell her that braiding threads or fibers is a *toladah* of *oreig*[123] and it is forbidden on Shabbos.

Potzei'a — Pulling Threads From Material

 What Is This Melachah, and How Was It Used in Building the Mishkan

I showed you the loom, but I didn't show you the woven sheets that were made into the *yerios*.

These are really special fabrics!

Oh no! There's a little hole here!

I'll run and tell my grandfather. He'll know how to fix it!

Saba! I found a hole in the *yerias ha'izim*!

Don't worry, Betzalel.

In order to fix the hole, I will pull a thread from another part of the fabric, and I'll use it to fill in the hole.[124]

The *melachah* of *potzei'a*: pulling threads from a woven fabric.

Unraveling a thread into fibers is included in this melachah.

Now, let's find the calendar page of the year you live in. You're going home!

What Is This Melachah, and How Was It Used in Building the Mishkan

Ow!

Oh no!

Did you get hurt?

I'm alright! Just a bruise and a scuffed shoe. Oh, and my lace tore!

What should we do? I don't like walking with untied laces!

You can tie the two parts of the lace together!

Good idea! But we have to make the knot very tight! I don't want it to come loose next time I trip...

Of course! A kesher shel kayama – a permanent knot!

Joining two things together with a permanent knot is the av melachah of kosheir.[125]

In the Mishkan, they tied together any threads of the yerios that tore during the weaving.

But what are these nets for?

They used nets to catch the chilazon, from which the techeiles dye was made. The hunters had to tie knots on the nets when making them.[126]

A Permanent Knot and a Temporary Knot

I finally organized all my stuff!

This bag has crafts from preschool, pieces of broken toys and lots of unmatched stuff.

I'm tying the sack shut, and I might never again open it!

A knot that you tie permanently, or one that you mean to keep tied indefinitely, is a kesher shel kayama, a permanent knot. The Torah forbids tying it on Shabbos.[127]

This bag has my tests, report cards, notes and things like that I'm tying it up now, but I think I'll want to look inside in a month or so.

If you tie a knot planning to untie it a long time later, it is a kesher shel kayama mid'Rabbanan.[128]

This bag has my nosh. I'll probably open it today! I'm tying the knot on this bag for less than a day!

A non-professional knot that you plan to untie within 24 hours is not a kesher shel kayama.[129]

Look at the next page to find out what is considered a kesher shel uman.

Kosheir

A Professional Knot

I need to open these packages. Can you help me?

Who tied this package? This is a really complicated knot!

Perhaps that is what is known as a *kesher shel uman*, a professional knot?

A *kesher shel uman* is a very strong knot that will not come apart on its own.

Because we don't know which knots are considered *kesher shel uman*, we must not tie any kind of strong knot. This is because it might be a professional knot that the Torah forbids on Shabbos.[130]

The cord on this package is tied with a double knot, or a *kesher al gabbei kesher*.

That is considered a strong knot that must not be tied on Shabbos.[131]

I finally got that knot open!

Now we have a great rope!

Did you notice the knot at the end of the rope? It looks like a very simple knot.

A knot at the end of a string is also considered strong even though it is a simple knot, it must not be tied on Shabbos.[132]

A Slipknot Over a Knot

Yossi, are you ready to go to shul?

I just need to tie my shoes, and I'm ready.

Did you tie them with a slipknot on top of a knot?

Of course, that's the way we tie shoes.[133]

I just hope you are not so lazy that you kick your shoes off without untying the bow!

What do you care whether I'm lazy?

Your habits are not what bothers me. It's something else altogether.

Although a slipknot is not a professio[nal] knot, if you leave it tied for too lon[g] it considered a *kesher shel kayama* t[hat] is forbidden on Shabbos!

Tying a slipknot on top a knot is permitted only if you untie it some time that day.[134]

So from now on, you'll make sure not to be lazy, right?

Kosheir

Knots We Can Tie on Shabbos

This bag keeps on opening up.

Soon, all these potato chips and other snacks are going to spill out!

Well, of course! You didn't tie it shut!

Of course I tied the bag shut! But it opened itself?

Sure, you tied it this way.

A single knot made from two ends of a string, or of a bag in this case, is neither a *kesher shel uman* nor a *kesher shel kayama.*

So we're allowed to tie such a knot on Shabbos?

Yes! As we have seen, it keeps on opening up and doesn't stay tied very long.[135]

There's another type of knot that we are allowed to make on Shabbos, because it is neither a permanent knot nor a *kesher shel uman.* It's called an *anivah,* a slipknot.[136]

Now, let's tie this bag of nosh professionally and make sure it stays closed.

Gezeirah of Chazal So You Won't Tie Knots

Oy! What happened to your sandal? Let's take it to the shoemaker!

Why run? I'll just tie the ends of the strap together...

And it's as good as new!

That's so interesting! Is this how they used to make shoes?

Yes. They tied straps to the bottom of the sole with a *kesher shel kayama.* I guess that this knot on my shoe decided not to be very *kayama.*

You know what? If the strap would have broken on Shabbos, I would not have been allowed to put it back in place, even if I don't tie it.

Why? Which *melachah* is that?

It's a *gezeirah* of Chazal.

Chazal ruled that no one may take any action that might lead him to tie a knot that is forbidden by the Torah.[137]

Normally, after putting the strap back in place, you tie it. That's why we are not even allowed to put it back. It might lead us to tie a knot.

What if the action I take might make me tie a knot that is forbidden *mid'Rabbanan?*

Chazal did not make a *gezeirah* forbidding that.[138]

53

Kosheir

Matir
Untying

Tightening an Existing Knot

What Is this Melachah, and How Was It Used in Building the Mishkan

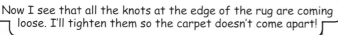

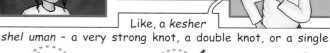

Tightening an existing knot is considered the melachah of kosheir. If you wouldn't tighten it, the knot might come loose. Therefore, tightening the knot is the same as tying.[139]

How can I connect these two sets of papers?

We've run out of staples and there are no more paper clips.

Maybe tape? Hey! Where did the tape go?

Do you know how we did it? We sewed them together with needle and thread!

Do you mean you sewed papers instead of material?

No, we sewed both paper and fabrics.

Well, once we're talking about sewing things, let's talk about the melachah of tofeir, sewing.

Great!

In the Mishkan they had to connect the yerios to make the Mishkan's covering. They did it by sewing them together.

The definition of tofeir: Connecting two things by making at least two stitches. This is forbidden on Shabbos.

And here is your set of papers, all put together. I hope the stitches hold!

Your pants cuff is coming down! You better have it fixed now!

Thanks for pointing it out. Right now it needs only a few stitches!

I think that two stitches will be enough.

Hey! The material doesn't hold onto the stitches. Why does the thread keep coming loose?

I'll try again.

It got loose again!

You forget to make a knot at the end of the thread, so the stitches come right out.

On Shabbos, it is forbidden to sew stitches that last.

And what about stitches that don't last, like mine?

Chazal forbade all sewing, even stitches that don't stay put.[141]

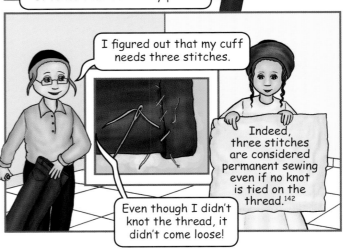
I figured out that my cuff needs three stitches.

Indeed, three stitches are considered permanent sewing even if no knot is tied on the thread.[142]

Even though I didn't knot the thread, it didn't come loose!

I finally bought a stapler, paper clips and tape!

Now, where did I put that pile of papers?

Oh, here it is! I'm going to take out the stitches and staple the pages!

What's wrong with having them connected with stitches?

I need to send them to someone. Nowadays, no one sews papers together.

I will be happier if they are stapled or taped together.

Do you know that taping, stapling and sewing are all considered the same melachah?

Really? Actually, they are very similar! All of those actions connect two things.

The *tolados* of *tofeir*: connecting pages or any other materials with staples[143] or glue.[144]

All these things are forbidden on Shabbos.

I have a lot of things that need mending!

The zipper on these pants is torn off.

A button is missing from each of these pairs.

Soon I won't have anything to wear!

I don't have any zippers or buttons, and I can wear all my clothes.

In those days, they tied things together, didn't they?

Yes.

And they used hooks and things like that.

But you know what? The zipper is an amazing invention! It makes it easy to connect two things!

Connecting two things...wait, isn't that what *tofeir* is?

A zipper, a button and Velcro connect two parts of a garment.

It is permissible to use those things on Shabbos because they are made to open and close all the time - whereas sewing and gluing connect things permanently.[145]

Toladah of the Melachah: Tightening Loose Stitches

Lately I need a lot of things fixed!

It didn't fall off; it's about to fall off, but maybe we can stop it.

Now this button fell off!

Super! It's all fixed!

Pull the thread that connects the button to the garment, and maybe it will move back into place!

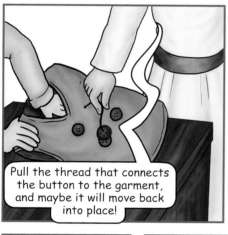

What did you say? Pull the loose thread...

Maybe we can save fixing this sleeve as well?

And it's all fixed! What a great idea!

This method doesn't always work. It's good for loose threads, not for torn threads.

On Shabbos we are not allowed to pull loose threads tight.

It is forbidden to pull a loose thread to tighten its stitches,[146] or to tighten the thread connecting a button to the garment.[147] This is a *toladah* of *tofeir*.

What Is this Melachah, and How Was It Used in Building the Mishkan

Can you help me tear this cloth?

Ready? Now pull!

But hold on now! Are you tearing this cloth because you are angry?

Not at all. I'm very calm and happy!

This is old material, and I have no use for it.

This fabric is tough! It won't let us tear it!

But you will definitely let me teach you about the *melachah* of *korei'a*, tearing.

Interesting! Why would they want to tear cloth to build the Mishkan? Tearing just ruins things.

Every so often, there was a hole in a *yeriah*. To fix it with a straight seam, they needed to tear the *yeriah* on both sides of the hole.[148]

Tearing apart or separating things that had been permanently connected is the *melachah* of *korei'a*.

Korei'a

Toladah of Korei'a

Detaching Papers From One Another

Winding up the Second Group of Melachos

What Is this Melachah, and How Was It Used in Building the Mishkan

What do you have there? Is it a present?

So why are you smiling?

No. It's a box of pictures!

Did you ever go fishing, Betzalel?

There were no rivers or lakes in the Midbar where we could fish, but in Mitzrayim we definitely fished in the Nile!

Because we've finished learning another group of *melachos*. That should make me and you happy!

And all our readers!

Here's a fishing rod. Let's see who will catch the first fish!

What do you plan to do with the fish?

I'll put them into a bucket with water. At home I'll put them into the aquarium my father bought me!

But there's another reason to be happy: There's another group of *melachos* waiting for us.

The Mishkan was covered with four types of coverings:
The *Yerios* of the Mishkan
Yerios Izim (goat hair)
Hides of *Eilim Me'odamim*
Hides of the *Techashim*

When you catch a fish, you take away its freedom. In the aquarium he will not be free to move around!

And that's not allowed?

The *melachos* that we learned until now had to do with preparing the *yerios*.

The *melachos* that we will learn now involve preparing the hides that were used for coverings.

Starting with shearing the wool and ending with sewing the cloth together to form a *yeriah*.

Well, it's forbidden on Shabbos.

The *melachah* of *tzad* is whatever a person does to take away an animal's freedom.[152]

For the Mishkan they trapped *eilim* (rams) and *techashim* in order to use their skins for the Mishkan's covers.

Trapping into a Place Where It Still Needs Catching

Why are you holding that bird?

I like the way it chirps. After trying a long time, I managed to catch it!

Where are you going to put it?

Are the windows and the door all closed?

Now I can let it loose in the house!

What good will it do you in the house?

In order to play with it, you'll have to run and catch it again!

But it's trapped in the house!

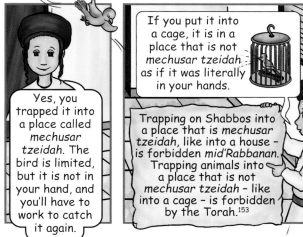

Yes, you trapped it into a place called *mechusar tzeidah*. The bird is limited, but it is not in your hand, and you'll have to work to catch it again.

If you put it into a cage, it is in a place that is not *mechusar tzeidah* as if it was literally in your hands.

Trapping on Shabbos into a place that is *mechusar tzeidah*, like into a house – is forbidden *mid'Rabbanan*. Trapping animals into a place that is not *mechusar tzeidah* – like into a cage – is forbidden by the Torah.[153]

Bemino Nitzod & Ein Bemino Nitzod (animals we hunt and those we don't)

I don't think we'll ever catch a big wild animal like...

Like a deer, for example!

And even if you really wanted a fox fur, you wouldn't go out on a hunting trip!

So we hardly ever do anything that has to do with the *melachah* of *tzad*!

That's not exactly true!

Ugh! This fly is really annoying!

Okay! I got it!

You caught it! Catching flies is included in the *melachah* of *tzad*!

However, catching flies is forbidden *only mid'Rabbanan*, because people do not usually hunt flies – *ein bemino nitzod*. The same applies to many kinds of butterflies and other bugs.[154]

But hunting animals that people normally hunt for – *bemino nitzod* – like a deer or a fox, is forbidden by the Torah.[155]

Now, set that fly free!

60

Tzad

Setting Up a Trap

What are you doing, Yossi?

I want to see what mice like to eat!

I found it! Hard cheese!

Are there mice in your home?

Lately I've found lots of chewed up papers and cloths. I'm afraid that a mouse has been visiting!

So let's set a trap for it!

We'll put a piece of cheese in it! to attract the mouse

This way we can trap it!

Why hasn't it come yet?

It's waiting for me to teach you that setting up a mousetrap on Shabbos is forbidden mid'Rabbanan,[156] because it catches mice.

I now permit the mouse to come!

Catching Domestic Animals

It's so nice to be in nature! You're used to it, aren't you?

Absolutely! We have to get this sheep back inside the corral.. Soon it will be dark!

But that is trapping it into a closed place! We're not allowed to!

A domesticated animal, which does not run away from people who come to catch it can be coaxed into a cage,[157] but the animal cannot be picked up because it is muktzeh.[158]

So we're allowed to coax this chicken into its coop also?

A chicken is a domesticated animal, but when it is outside, it tends to run away from anyone who comes to catch it.

Mid'Rabbanan it is forbidden to catch such animals on Shabbos.[159]

So this chicken will stay outside?

Don't worry. Chickens usually come back to their coop by themselves. No one has to bring them.*

But now let's coax ourselves back home. It's time to get ready for seudah shlishis.

* According to the Mechabeir, chickens are the same as other domesticated animals and it is permissible to catch them.

61

Tzad

Shocheit
Slaughtering

Trapping Dangerous Animals

Do you see what I see?

I'm afraid so!

That's a snake out there!

We have to call a snake catcher right away! It might be poisonous!

Even if the snake is not poisonous, we should have it caught!

But it can't kill anyone!

It can't kill but it can bite and cause injury and that's why we are allowed to catch snakes even on Shabbos!

We are allowed to catch snakes on Shabbos?

You are allowed to catch a non-poisonous snake,[160] if your purpose is to stop it from hurting people.

A poisonous snake may be trapped and even killed, because it is pikuach nefesh![161]

How It Was Used in Building the Mishkan

I'm going to the store to buy a chicken. Do you want to come with me?

Sure! And I'll go with you to the shocheit!

When I buy chicken, it's already slaughtered, salted, rinsed and kashered!

So you've never seen a chicken being shechted?

I guess not!

Not only have I seen chickens being shechted, I also saw the eilim and techashim slaughtered for the Mishkan!

The eilim and techashim were slaughtered in order to use their skins for the Mishkan covers.

Shechitah, the slaughter of animals, is forbidden on Shabbos.

Here's the store with chickens already shechted

GROCERY

62

Shocheit

Shocheit

Mafshit
Skinning

Me'abeid
Tanning

What Is this Melachah, and How Was It Used in Building the Mishkan

Kashering Meat

Hey, I made a mistake! My mother asked me to buy ten pounds of sugar.

And you bought ten pounds of salt...

You didn't put the bags of salt away?

No, we're going to kasher chickens!

What can we do with all this salt? It will take at least half a year to use it up!

There are more ways to use salt besides flavoring food and dipping bread into it

Like what?

I already asked your father to be our *mashgiach*.

You've probably done this before!

That's right. We didn't buy chicken at the store. It takes a long time to kasher a chicken and I've watched the process more than once.

Like tanning skins! After the skin was taken off the ram's body, it needed to be processed so it could be used.

So they salted it and soaked it in lime or other chemicals.

But Betzalel, why are you putting salt all over the chicken?

To pull out the blood from the meat, because we are not allowed to eat blood![169]

The *melachah* of *me'abeid*, tanning skins with salt or chemicals, is forbidden on Shabbos.[168]

So let's run and bring this salt to your grandfather!

No, let's keep it!

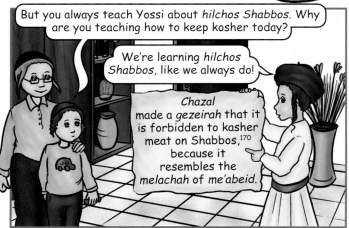

But you always teach Yossi about *hilchos Shabbos*. Why are you teaching how to keep kosher today?

We're learning *hilchos Shabbos*, like we always do!

Chazal made a *gezeirah* that it is forbidden to kasher meat on Shabbos,[170] because it resembles the *melachah* of *me'abeid*.

Salting Vegetables – Me'abeid With Food

We've salted the chickens, kashered them, cooked them, and ate – and there's still salt left!

We can salt and pickle vegetables! Have you ever tried that?

No, but we'll try now! Let's fill the windowsill with lots of jars!

And we'll have pickled cucumbers, pickled onions, pickled peppers, and pickled radishes!

But we'll have to wait to do it on Sunday! Today is Erev Shabbos and there's no chance we'll have time!

On Shabbos, although being me'abeid food is not forbidden by the Torah, Chazal forbid us to change foods by salting them.

That is why we cannot salt vegetables in order to pickle them.[171]

So I'm not allowed to salt my salad on Shabbos?

The salad is also seasoned with oil, right? The nature of oil is to weaken the effect of the salt. But it's better to pour the oil into the salad before you sprinkle in the salt.[172]

We are not allowed to season salad with salt alone on Shabbos.

What Is this Melachah, and How Was It Used in Building the Mishkan

Oops!

Look at your shoes!

The latest style mud coated shoe

You can use a knife to scrape the mud off!

You should do it quickly before the mud dries.

But I'm afraid I might scrape the leather!

You're right. By scraping a shoe with a knife, you peel and smooth its surface.

Smooth it? What do you mean?

The melachah of memacheik in the Mishkan means to scrape leather's surface smooth.

After the skins were tanned in the Mishkan, they were scraped smooth to remove any hair or wool.

Take care not to scrape your shoe's surface

It is forbidden on Shabbos Shabbos to do this.[173]

Because this is the melachah of memacheik.

Uh, oh! The china closet was left open!

All the silver is tarnished! Look at this *becher*!

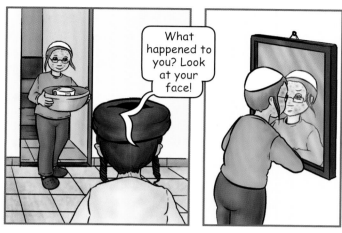

What happened to you? Look at your face!

And the menorah! And the candlesticks!

How come we didn't notice that the door wasn't closed?

Judging by the way the silver looks, it must have been open for a few days already!

During the night some mosquitoes decided to bite me all over my face!

Here's a cream to soothe the itching. Do you want to use it?

Yes, thanks!

So let's go! We have some soft rags and polish. Let's start shining it!

When we polish silver – we are smoothing its surface and buffing it.

But what will you do if the mosquitoes bite you on Shabbos? You are not allowed to rub on cream during Shabbos because of *memacheik*.[175]

Maybe I can spread the cream on a bandage on Friday and then put it on the bites on Shabbos?

This is similar to the smoothing of the skins done for the Mishkan. That is why it is forbidden on Shabbos, as a *toladah* of *memacheik*.[174]

Great! We've finished polishing!

Now let's put all these things back in their place. This time, we won't forget to the close the door, that's for sure!

We must not spread creams on Shabbos.

Chazal decreed that it is forbidden to use a bandage with cream spread on it, so we won't spread cream on Shabbos.[176]

So let's go! We're going to buy mosquito repellent!

If a person is bedridden with a non-life-threatening illness, he may put on a bandage that had cream spread on it before Shabbos. He may also ask a non-Jew to spread cream for him on a bandage on Shabbos, or he can do it himself with a *shinui*.[177]

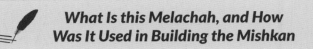

Hey! It's Shabbos!

Yes, I know it's Shabbos! That's why I'm preparing *seudah shlishis* for us!

What are these papers?

These papers all didn't come out good!

I'm trying to write a letter on unlined paper, and the lines are coming out so crooked!

So why are you spreading butter on the challah?

You told me not long ago that we're not allowed to spread creams on Shabbos!

Because *memacheik* does not apply to food. You're allowed to spread butter on Shabbos.

So score the lines before you write.

How do I do that?

Take a look at this picture!

But aren't you smoothing the butter on the challah!

My intention is not to make the butter smooth on the challah. I just want to have the slice of challah covered with butter.

That is why it is permitted on Shabbos.[178]

This is my grandfather scoring straight lines on the skins. These lines are guides so that he can then cut the skin exactly the way he needs it.

The lines we score on the paper will guide your writing.

Here's a bowl of tuna salad. I want to smooth the top of the salad down. Am I allowed to do that also?

In this case, your purpose is to make the surface smooth so that it should look nicer, so it's better to be strict and not to do it on Shabbos.[179]

The page is ready! Now I'll have no problem writing in straight lines.

The *melachah* of *mesarteit*: scoring paper or parchment so you can write straight lines[180] or so that you can cut in straight lines.[181]

This is forbidden on Shabbos.

Scoring Lines on Food

Would you like an orange?

Yes, thanks!

As soon as I finish peeling it, you can have the delicious fruit!

Why did you cut lines in the orange peel?

Why shouldn't I? This way it is easy to peel it!

But you're not allowed to score lines on Shabbos. It's *mesarteit*!

I didn't forget, Yossi.

We are allowed to mark lines on a fruit or a cake with a knife so that you can cut even slices.

It is not forbidden to be *mesarteit* on foods if you are doing it for the sake of eating them..[182]

What Is this Melachah, and How Was It Used in Building the Mishkan

I've finally figured out how big to make this sign!

I already marked straight lines to guide me, and now I'm going to cut it.

So you're cutting the paper to an exact size and shape, using scissors.

That's right! Exactly what I told you!

I repeated your words because the *melachah* of *mechateich*, which is forbidden on Shabbos, means to cut something into an exact size or shape.[183]

For the Mishkan they cut the skins after measuring and scoring them. Then they spread the skins over the Mishkan.

What if I want to cut a piece of paper for a sign, but I don't care what shape or size it is?

What if I want to cut papers just for the sake of cutting them, and I don't care about any size or shape?

As long as you have some purpose in cutting, it is forbidden on Shabbos even if you don't care about the size or shape of the pieces, because of the *melachah* of *korei'a*, tearing.[184]

Chazal made a *gezeirah* forbidding this, too,[185] because of the *melachah* of *korei'a*.

Slicing Food; and Winding up the Third Group of Melachos for Hides

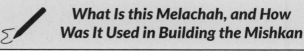

What Is this Melachah, and How Was It Used in Building the Mishkan

I measured lines to slice the cake.

I want each slice to be the same size!

Wait! Isn't cutting to an exact size included in *mechateich*?

Why not slice the cake without measuring? This way, I might get a bigger slice!

The melachah of *mechateich* doesn't apply to food. Therefore we can cut food on Shabbos to an exact size.[186]

But remember not to chop the food into very tiny pieces because of the *melachah* of *tochein*.[187]

What's this carton for? Are you planning to put the slices of cake into it?

It's better to put them in a plastic container!

I'm packing up the pictures we used until now into the carton.

We've finished another group of *melachos* – all those involved in processing the hides.

Can you bring me an inkwell, ink, and a quill?

But my father is not a *sofer*! We don't have those items at home!

So how do you write? Oh, I know, you write with pens, but I'm not used to writing with a pen.

What do you want to write?

I want to write on parchment the what the *melachah* of *koseiv* means. We will start learning about it today: Writing letters.

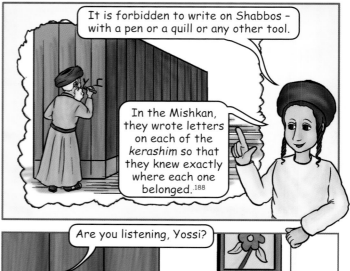

It is forbidden to write on Shabbos – with a pen or a quill or any other tool.

In the Mishkan, they wrote letters on each of the *kerashim* so that they knew exactly where each one belonged.[188]

Are you listening, Yossi?

Hmmm... sort of. I'm busy preparing a little surprise for you:

My uncle is a *sofer Sta"m*, and he said you can borrow a quill, inkwell, and ink from his house!

Writing That Lasts

Writing That Doesn't Last

Yossi, what things can you write on?

What's the question? On paper, on parchment, on a wooden board, on...

Sometimes, I write on the wall!

Mommy doesn't let you!

What are you working so hard on?

Water spilled on the table, and I'm trying to form letters with it.

What do you use to write?

You know that already. We can use pens, pencils, crayons, markers, and more

We can write with shoe polish, too!

Oops! All that I wrote just disappeared!

Of course! Writing with water does not last.

Did you try that on the walls, also?

The materials you said that you can write on, and all the things you said that you write with, make long-lasting writing.

Writing that lasts long is forbidden on Shabbos by the Torah.[189]

Oh, so now you are writing with water?

I'm writing on the steam condensed on the window.

It's actually fun!

The writing on the window also doesn't last.

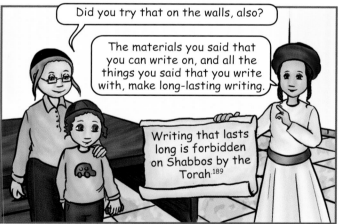

And if I write with a pen on... a leaf from a tree?

Although the writing lasts, the leaf rots quickly and does not last, so it is only forbidden mid'Rabbanan.[190]

Chazal made a gezeirah forbidding writing on Shabbos even if it can't last, if the writing is legible.[191]

Describing the shape of letters in the air is not considered writing at all. It is permitted on Shabbos.

Writing with a Shinui

Who wrote this? Your little brother?

No! I wrote it!

So why are the letters so crooked?

My right hand is bandaged so I had to write with my left hand, and this is how it came out!

Dear Friend Refuah Sheleimah! From Yossi

Writing with the hand that you don't usually write with is not allowed on Shabbos, mid'Rabbanan.[192]

Writing k'lachar yad – holding the pen backwards – is also forbidden on Shabbos, mid'Rabbanan.[193]

Even though the letters are neat and clear!

Dear Yossi Get Well soon! Betzalel

I think the ink has run out!

Take another pen and go over the letters again!

Writing over letters that are already written is also forbidden* on Shabbos.[194]

*see footnote to know if it is d'Oraisa or mid'Rabbanan.

Toladah of the Melachah of Koseiv

Who are you making paintings for?

I noticed that my room seems bare. There are no pictures on the walls.

So I decided to paint some pictures myself!

I drew this one with a pencil;

This one with colored pencils;

And for this one I used a pen.

Then I painted them all with gouache!

Now, instead of writing 'BOYS' on the door, we can write 'Painting Gallery'!

That's right! That's exactly what I wrote on this sign that I'm preparing!

You wrote and you drew pictures on the sign. Both are included in the melachah of koseiv.

Drawing pictures is a toladah of koseiv, and it is forbidden on Shabbos.[195]

Chazal's Gezeirah About Buying and Selling on Shabbos

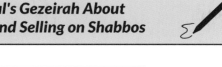

Where is my yarmulke?

I can't go to shul wearing this one!

Can't you borrow a yarmulke from someone?

My brother's yarmulke is too small, and you don't use the same kind that I do!

Wait! Our neighbors have a yarmulke store in their house! Maybe I'll buy one from them and I'll pay for it after Shabbos!

We can't! it is forbidden to buy anything on Shabbos – even if we don't pay that day.

Chazal made a *gezeirah* forbidding us to sell, buy, hire, or rent things on Shabbos, since we usually write a bill of sale.[196]

Hey Yossi! We found it!

Hey! How did my yarmulke get on your head?

I wanted to be big!

Gezeirah of Chazal About Weighing and Measuring on Shabbos

Can you measure how tall I am?

Sure, but why?

I want to know if I've grown this past year!

Just see if your pants became short...

I'll measure you anyway, but why are you standing on the scale?

Because I also want to see how much I weigh.

This is a very accurate scale.

We didn't have scales like that. Ours worked with weights.

I once saw such a scale at the *shuk*! You put the fruit on one side, and a weight on the other.

That's right. That's how we know how much the fruit weighs and how much it costs.

Chazal allowed us to weigh and measure on Shabbos for a mitzvah.[198]

People usually weigh or measure when buying things, so *Chazal* made a *gezeirah* forbidding any weighing or measuring on Shabbos.[197]

Mocheik
Erasing

Why is the table full of these strange bits of dirt?

I'm erasing and those bits rub off the eraser!

You're erasing so much. You made so many mistakes?

They are not mistakes. I'm erasing a school workbook that my big brother once used.

After I erase what he wrote, I can use it again.

So you're erasing in order to write!

In the Mishkan they also erased letters that were written on the *kerashim* by mistake, in order to write the correct letters there.

What you are doing exactly fits the definition of *mocheik*.

It is also the av melachah: Erasing something written in order to write something else in its place.[199]

Now that I've finished explaining, I can help you to erase it. Your hand must be really hurting by now!

I have a challenge for you: Try to open this ice pop without tearing the letters!

It's impossible! This wrapper is full of letters and writing on every side! There isn't one drop of clear space!

So on Shabbos you will not be able to open it and eat it, because by opening it you would tear the letters, and that is like erasing!

Tearing letters or pictures is like erasing, so it is forbidden on Shabbos.[200]

But there are lots of foods with wrappers that have letters!

This apple!

And this egg has a stamp!

And – hey! All the packages of nosh are full of letters!

They are! That's why we have to be very careful not to cut or tear letters when opening packages that we are allowed to open.[201]

Mocheik

Boneh
Building

Cutting Letters on Food

What Is this Melachah, and How Was It Used in Building the Mishkan

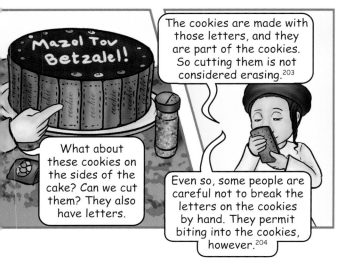

75

Boneh

Activities That Are Considered Boneh

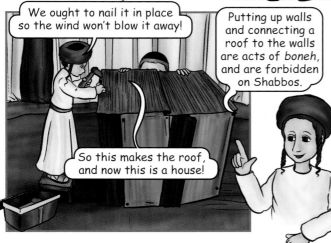

Making Repairs

Boneh

What's a Building? What's a Keli?

The melachah of boneh applies to buildings like this house, and also to *keilim* - tools and utensils.

Which things do you call buildings, Yossi?

A sukkah, a private house, a hut, an apartment building.

Which things do you call *keilim*?

A pot, broom, salt shaker, box, hammer - why do you ask?

Let me finish asking my questions and then it will be your turn.

What about a free-standing closet? Is it a building or a utensil?

It's like a building but it's not one. I don't know!

The halachah considers a building to be something that is connected to the ground, no matter what size it is.

How big is 40 se'ah?

Like this big cupboard:

It covers the space of three cubic *amos*.

The rules of *binyan* for keilim apply to articles that are not connected to the ground and are smaller than 40 se'ah. Anything larger than that has the same rules as a building.[209]

Boneh of Keilim

You painted the walls! It's so bright and cheery!

And you also put in a cabinet for our beautiful little house? So nice!

I only have to put the shelves into it and we can use it.

We don't need any screws or nails: the shelf rests on these pegs.

So today, we're not building at all!

Oh, but we are. Since this cabinet is bigger than 40 se'ah it is considered a building.

For a building, even setting things in place loosely on Shabbos is forbidden, like placing shelves in a cabinet.

But the broom has come off the stick!

We just have to sweep the floor and – we're finished.

So that's a perfect example of *binyan b'keilim*, building a tool.

We connect the stick to the broom by screwing it on very tightly.

Binyan b'keilim: On Shabbos you are not allowed to screw things very tightly together or nail them together.[210]

Boneh

Where are you taking all that?

My mother lets us eat supper in our private house.

Is that modeling clay?

I don't know what modeling clay is. This is called *cheimar*!

Oh, so you're playing with *cheimar*. Let me play with you!

Such a nice variety of food!

But I can't open these jars!

The covers are screwed shut too tightly!

I'm not playing. I'm making dishes!

You can form *cheimar* into different shapes and containers: I made a plate, a cup, a bowl and now I'm making a pitcher!

Screwed shut? Hold on!

Do you mean to say that I'm not allowed to screw covers onto jars on Shabbos, like screwing the stick into the broom?

But can you really use these? Won't they fall apart?

After shaping the containers, you leave them in the sun to dry.

And then you can use the dish until it breaks...

A container with a screw-on cover may be opened and closed on Shabbos because that is the regular way to use that container.[211]

But a broom and its stick are meant to remain connected.

Here's more important information: I managed to open the jars! What can I offer you?

That's very interesting! My friends and I never make dishes like this. The ones we use are made in a factory.

So now you know that you can make your own things!

Shaping dishes is a *toladah* of *meleches boneh* and it is forbidden on Shabbos.[212]

Boneh

Making an Ohel – a Tent

I thought that the house we built would be enough for you! What are you building now?

I'm not really building; I'm putting up a tent! But actually, putting up a tent is a *toladah* of *boneh*.

A tent?! How nice! Like Avraham Avinu? With four openings?

But where will you make the doorways? I see only the covering!

You're thinking of a tent that has a roof and walls, but even putting up a roof alone is enough to transgress the *melachah* of *boneh*.

The main purpose of a tent – a roof – is to protect from sun or rain.

So the material that you spread here is called an *ohel*, is that right?

In most cases, the roof is considered an *ohel* even though there are no walls.[213]

A Permanent Tent and a Temporary Tent

That's all? You're taking it apart already?

We're going inside. It's starting to get dark!

This tent was a temporary *ohel*. A tent that is meant to last for a long time is called a permanent *ohel*.

The tents in which we lived in the desert stood for a long time.

Actually, your tents were really like houses!

Indeed, putting up a permanent *ohel* is like building a house – even though we don't put pieces together.

The Torah forbids putting up a permanent *ohel* on Shabbos.

But if guests arrive on Shabbos and we want more space, we're allowed to make a temporary extension to our tent.

A temporary extension: An extension of an *ohel* that is not meant to stay in place very long.[214]

Boneh

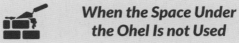

80

Boneh

A Temporary Mechitzah

This flashlight hardly makes any light!

We can't know that unless we darken the room!

But there is no door here.

Let's put up a *mechitzah*! We'll hang this blanket across the doorway on the hooks on the wall. Then the room will be dark!

Now I see that the flashlight works great!

We can take down the blanket now.

This was a very temporary *mechitzah*!

We are allowed to put up a temporary *mechitzah* on Shabbos – even if it is for the purpose of darkening the room.[218]

What if I want a permanent partition here?

You mean you want to put up a partition in a way that it can stay up for a long time? We are not allowed to put up a permanent partition on Shabbos.[219]

But you don't make those decisions in this house anyway, right?

Mechitzah Hamaterres

Did you see that strange sukkah?

Someone either didn't finish building it or didn't finish taking it apart.

I don't know, but in either case, it's not kosher now. It has only two walls!

That's easy to fix! We just have to add one wall. If we can get the wall to stand in place, it's kosher even without nails!

That wall changes it from a nonkosher sukkah to a kosher one.

A partition that changes something to make it kosher is called a *mechitzah hamaterres*.[220]

It is forbidden to put up a *mechitzah hamatteres* on Shabbos even if it is meant to stand for a short time.[220]

Don't we always put up a kosher sukkah before Sukkos begins?

Sure. But suppose a wall fell down or was knocked down by the wind. We have to know that we can't put up a wall and make it kosher on Shabbos or Yom Tov.

We've barely had a chance to use our house and you're taking it apart?

I decided to move it to another place. The sun hits it too hard over here.

So you're taking apart the house in order to build it again.

It is forbidden on Shabbos to demolish a building in order to rebuild it.

This melachah (soseir) was needed for the Mishkan as well:

They took the Mishkan apart in order to rebuild it in a different place.

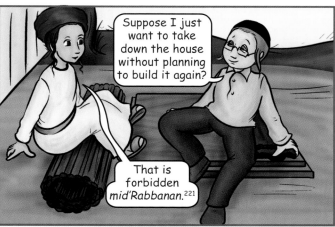

Suppose I just want to take down the house without planning to build it again?

That is forbidden mid'Rabbanan.[221]

When you taught me about boneh, we spent many lessons explaining the activities included in the melachah. What activities are included in the melachah of soseir?

We have a simple, short rule: Whatever the Torah forbids because of boneh, the Torah forbids taking apart because of soseir.

Just like we are not allowed to fix any part of a building –

We are also not allowed to take apart part of a building.

Just like we cannot put up a tent on Shabbos –

we may not take it down on Shabbos either.[222]

Just like we are not allowed to assemble tools or utensils –

We are not allowed to take apart such tools and utensils.[223]

Just like we cannot assemble utensils on Shabbos because of boneh, we cannot take them apart because of soseir.

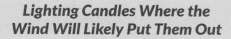

Do you smell what I smell?

Something's burning, that's for sure! But what is it?

Why did you open all the windows?

Why? Because there's no air in here! It's stuffy!

Oy! My mother asked me to turn off the flame under the pot of chicken.

I totally forgot about it!

But the chicken doesn't look cooked enough. So could it be burnt?

But look what happened! All the candles went out!

Oy...But why did you light candles?

Today is my grandfather's *yahrtzeit*. My father lit a *yahrtzeit* candle, and the wind blew it out!

I forgot two things. I was supposed to lower the flame an hour ago, and turn it off now.

Although you forgot two things, you stated in one sentence two actions that are included in the *melachah* we are going to learn about today:

The *melachah* of *mechabeh*: We are not allowed to extinguish, or put out a fire on Shabbos, and we are also not allowed to lower a flame on Shabbos.[224]

For the Mishkan, they put out fires in order to make coals from wood.

Okay, I'll close the windows and you can light the candles again.

When the wind blows on Shabbos I know that I have to be careful not to open windows or a door facing the Shabbos candles, because we are not allowed to cause the fire to go out.[225]

What about when the wind isn't blowing?

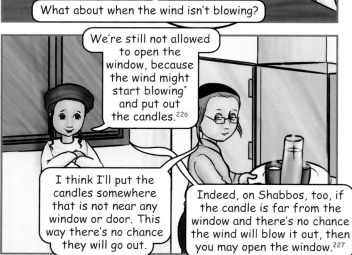

We're still not allowed to open the window, because the wind might start blowing* and put out the candles.[226]

I think I'll put the candles somewhere that is not near any window or door. This way there's no chance they will go out.

Indeed, on Shabbos, too, if the candle is far from the window and there's no chance the wind will blow it out, then you may open the window.[227]

*If you really need to, you can be lenient and open the window slowly and carefully.

Making a Fire Go Out By Itself

Wow!! Look at that thick smoke!

It's not only smoke! That apartment is burning!

Why are you smiling? Did you think of a joke?

I remembered a story that once happened to us. It's not very funny, but its on the subject we're talking about!

One Shabbos, I was learning with my grandfather by candlelight.

All the people are running out of the building! Look!

Of course! It's very dangerous to stay inside!

I'm afraid! And we're not allowed to put fire out on Shabbos!

Our lamp somehow got knocked over, and the tablecloth began to burn.

And here comes the fire truck! Look how much water it's spraying!

I hope they'll get the fire under control. There are many buildings in the area. The fire might spread and put people's lives in danger!

Take it easy, Betzalel! Its just a little fire, and we can arrange for it to go out. It is permissible to indirectly make a fire to go out on Shabbos.

We'll put pitchers full of water near the fire. When the fire breaks them, the water will put it out.[230]

But first, let's try another way: We'll pour water around the fire, and when the fire reaches it, it will go out.[231]

If a fire breaks out on Shabbos in a place where people live, if there is a question of *pikuach nefesh*, one may call the fire department and put out the fire.[228]

But if the fire breaks out in a place where there is no danger to anyone's life, then even though a lot of property will be lost no one may put the fire out on Shabbos.[229]

And indeed, the fire went out!

My grandfather then reviewed the halachos: We resort to indirectly putting a fire out only when no one's life is in danger. When there might be danger, one may put out the fire directly.

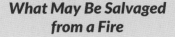

What May Be Salvaged from a Fire

What Is this Melachah, and How Was It Used in Building the Mishkan

What a nightmare!

We were just talking about fires and I'm dreaming about them at night!

I was in a building that was on fire, and I wanted to save as much as possible, but I didn't know what to grab first.

I wanted to take everything!!

This is my menorah. My father lights his with oil, but I light mine with candles.

How do you make the fire?

Simple! I strike a match and use it to light the *shammash* candle.

And then I noticed a pile of *seforim*. I took them and ran outside into...

Into my bed!

You saved the really important stuff!

Even on Shabbos we are allowed to save *seforim* from a fire!

Oh, so you use the match to ignite fire.

And then you use the match to light the *shammash*.

Right. And once I light the *shammash* I use it to light the other candles.

We can't save other things?

Chazal were afraid that if a person starts running to save his belongings, he might forget it is Shabbos, and he will put out a fire when it is forbidden.

So they made a *gezeirah* that it is permitted to save only the following items[232]:

I also have an interesting riddle for you: Why didn't they light Chanukah candles in the Mishkan?

The *melachah* of *mav'ir* forbids making things burn in any way: striking a match, making an existing fire bigger, or using an existing fire to make another fire on Shabbos.[236]

I never thought about that. Is that true? They didn't?

You may take as much food and dishes that you need for that Shabbos.[233]

It is permitted to take clothes needed for that Shabbos. But you are allowed to put on many sets of clothing on top of one another and save them all.[234]

And of course, as I already told you, we are allowed to save *kisvei kodesh*, holy writings.[235]

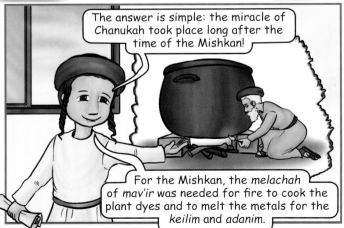

The answer is simple: the miracle of Chanukah took place long after the time of the Mishkan!

For the Mishkan, the *melachah* of *mav'ir* was needed for fire to cook the plant dyes and to melt the metals for the *keilim* and *adanim*.

Mav'ir

Making Fire Bigger on Shabbos

The oil is almost all burned up.! I want my lights to burn longer so I can enjoy looking at the flame!

By adding oil, I do not make the fire bigger, but I make it continue burning longer.
That is not allowed on Shabbos because of mav'ir.

So add more oil!

But there are ways to make a fire grow bigger, like---

I can't really show this to you, so imagine that this is happening:

There is a small fire in the middle of the room, and I want to make it bigger.

Okay, and its also possible to open the door or the window so that the wind will make the fire grow.

We can add more wood or oil!

But wind puts out fire. That's why you told me that we're not allowed to open the door on Shabbos!

The wind will blow out a small fire like a candle.

But with a larger fire, the wind fans the flames and makes them grow bigger.

Therefore, we may not open the door or window facing a fire, and this time because of mav'ir.[237]

We can open it if there is no wind blowing,[238] or if the fire is very far from the window or door and there's no chance of the wind reaching the fire.[239]

Gezeirah of Chazal: "Shemma Yateh"

What are you studying when it's so late?

I try to learn two halachos in Sefer Shemiras Halashon every day.

But it's dark here. How are you able to read?

I have a night light that I prepared before Shabbos. It's focused right over the sefer!

In our tent, we didn't have electric lamps, of course. We learned by the light of an oil lamp.

But I couldn't read by its light by myself on Shabbos.

Why? It didn't make enough light?

It did, but sometimes the wick burned down and we needed to tip the lamp to bring the oil to the wick. That is why Chazal forbid reading by the light of an oil lamp on Shabbos.[240]

Two people may learn together,[241] or I could ask someone to be a 'shomer' to make sure that I wouldn't forget and tip the lamp.[242]

We use paraffin candles! They burn beautifully and they never need to be tipped!

That's right. And that is why it is permitted to read by the light of wax candles[243] or by the light of an electric bulb.[244]

86

Mav'ir

Electric Appliances with a Heating Element

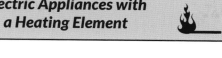

It's c-c-cold...

Here's a space heater.

Come sit next to it and warm your frozen feet!

It feels good here.

This heater reminds me of what we had. But we filled ours with wood.

All that's missing is the smell of fire and the crackling noise.

When you use a wood oven like yours, which has real fire inside, you are doing the *melachah* of *mav'ir*, right?

Yes. But when you turn on an electric heater like this, the heating element gets red hot, and that's also the *melachah* of *mav'ir*.

We have other appliances that become red when they are on: an electric stove burner! The liver roaster! And sometimes even our baking oven!

We are not allowed to turn on any of these devices on Shabbos because of *mav'ir*.[245]

Some electric appliances work without a heating element.

Look ahead to the next column!

Electric Appliances

I notice that you have a few kinds of lamps:

A long lamp like that, which shines bright,

Round bulbs, and all kinds of other bulbs.

A pear shaped bulb,

It's not only the shape that is different, right?

That's true. Some bulbs have a metal filament inside. It gets red hot when we turn it on.

And other bulbs work work differently. But I'm not an electrician so I can't tell you exactly how...

And your appliances? I saw that some of them have a cord that connects them to the wall, and some don't connect to the wall!

There are devices that are connected to an outlet – to a source of electricity in the wall,

And there are some that have batteries in the device itself.

But why are you asking me all this? I told you that I don't know how electricity works!

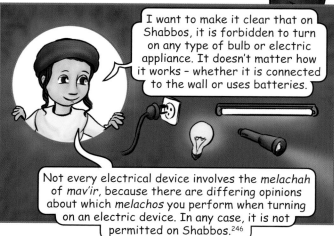

I want to make it clear that on Shabbos, it is forbidden to turn on any type of bulb or electric appliance. It doesn't matter how it works – whether it is connected to the wall or uses batteries.

Not every electrical device involves the *melachah* of *mav'ir*, because there are differing opinions about which *melachos* you perform when turning on an electric device. In any case, it is not permitted on Shabbos.[246]

Bathing on Shabbos

I'm cold! Even this cup of tea doesn't make me warm!

I feel like having a hot shower now. But actually...

Right after the shower, I'll be cold again! So never mind!

There's a much more important reason not to shower today:

Chazal made a *gezeirah* forbidding bathing your whole body or most of it on Shabbos in hot water.

I know that we are not allowed to heat water on Shabbos, but what if the water was heated on Erev Shabbos?

In our times, when there was no shower at home, people bathed in bathhouses. Sometimes, the bathouse owners would heat the water on Shabbos, and claimed that they heated it before Shabbos.[249]

What if I want only to wash my hands or feet with water that was heated before Shabbos?

Chazal made it forbidden to bathe one's whole body in hot water, even if it was heated before Shabbos.

Chazal did not forbid washing one's face, hands and feet in water heated before Shabbos[247] but you may not squeeze water from your hair.

What Is this Melachah, and How Was It Used in Building the Mishkan

We spoke about a *patish*, a hammer, in the *melachah* of *boneh*!

What does it say here? *Meleches makkeh bepatish*?

This is a totally different type of hammering! It's not hammering to break things or to knock in a nail!

For the Mishkan, after they fashioned all the *keilim*, they often found that some were lopsided or a bit crooked.

So, using a hammer, they banged on the *keli* until the shape was perfect.

Very interesting. I always knew that we use hammers to break things. I didn't know we could use them to fix things!

But is hitting with a hammer the only way to finish making a utensil?

There are other actions that are included in this *melachah*.

Although in the Mishkan they used a hammer to finish making *keilim* the *melachah* applies to an action that finishes or completes a *keli*.[248]

It's Wednesday, right?

Yes, that's right!

So why are you wearing this fancy suit?

Why are you giving me funny looks?

Something looks wrong. Something is crooked!

My brother is getting married soon and I'm trying on my new suit.

Who sewed this suit?

I don't know. We bought it in a store.

But what difference does it make?

Oh! Your glasses are bent out of shape!

That's no big deal. It's very simple to straighten these metal frames.

I don't even need to go to the optician to do it!

Whoever sewed the suit did not finish the final step.

Why? What's wrong?

He finished sewing the suit together.

I just bend the frame to the right,

And I'm done!

And then to the left –

You know, Yossi, that even though you didn't need a professional to straighten your glasses – you are not allowed to do it on Shabbos because of *makkeh bepatish*.

But he didn't remove these leftover bits of thread.

This is the final step to complete the making of your suit, so it must not be done on Shabbos because of *makkeh bepatish*.[250]

In order for the garment to be totally finished and perfect to wear, you need to cut off or pull out these threads.

Is it forbidden to straighten any bent item on Shabbos?

On Shabbos we are not allowed to make any repairs. We cannot straighten a crooked spoon or the tines of a fork that are bent out of shape, because that makes them more fit for use.[251]

Separating Terumos and Ma'asaros

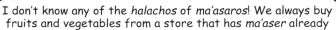

Tevilas Keilim

Makkeh Bepatish

 Folding Laundry

 Lacing Shoes

Why do you throw your clothes into your closet that way? It's a mess!

I don't see any need to fold them!

No one sees what's on my shelves inside mycloset.

Uh, oh! I forgot to put laces on my new shoes!

If I can do it quickly I'll get to davening on time!

No, don't!

It's forbidden to put new laces on shoes since they are meant to stay for a long time. That's what makes the shoes ready to be worn.[256]

I guess tomorrow you will understand...You'll find that your clothes are all wrinkled when you take them out to wear them!

Nowadays people do not iron clothes by folding them them.

You have an iron that does that job very well.

Baruch Hashem you stopped me in time! But now what will I do? My old shoe is totally torn!

Do you have any green, red, or orange laces?

First of all, I don't. But even if I did, how would Purim-colored laces help?

If there's no question that you will remove the new laces after Shabbos, you may put those laces on your shoes on Shabbos.[257]

Wait, what about this shoe?

I don't know. It belonged to my brother, but I think it fits me now!

But the shoelace came out of this shoe also!

In ancient times, we used to fold our clothes very carefully, stretching the material to take away all the wrinkles.

That was the final stage of laundering them so they were ready to wear!

Therefore, Chazal made a gezeirah forbidding folding laundry on Shabbos, because doing so looks like fixing the clothes for use.[254]

With some garments, there is no difference if they are folded or not because they don't wrinkle. One example is towels!

Things made of fabric that is not affected by folding may be folded on Shabbos.[255]

There are other situations when it is permissible to fold laundry on Shabbos, but you have to find out the custom in your house!

You are allowed to put back a lace on a shoe if it had already been there.

But if it's hard to put on the shoelace because the holes in the shoe are too small, or because the plastic came off the ends, so you have to really work hard to get it in[258] – then it is forbidden on Shabbos in all cases.

Makkeh Bepatish

Makkeh Bepatish Regarding Food

Now I understand that the *melachah* of *makkeh bepatish* makes it forbidden to finish any article to make it usable on Shabbos.

But we always fix other things besides tools, clothes, and shoes, and make them ready for use!

Like...

What about food and drinks?

The beverage concentrate is not ready to drink. You have to add water to make it.

The baby's cereal also isn't ready to use. You have to add milk or water so that it should be completely "fixed".

But we make drinks on Shabbos! And we mix cereal while making sure to avoid the *melachos* of *losh* and *bishul*!

Yes, we do.

Because *makkeh bepatish* does not apply to food and drinks.[259]

Opening Packages

What's this mountain? What's it for?

Our delivery just arrived! Let's put it away together.

There are so many types of packages here. There are paper packages, plastic containers cartons, cans, and jars.

I'm sure that in the desert you had only wooden barrels and earthen jugs, right?

But how do you open all these packages and boxes?

Each packaging is opened differently: some by hand and others with a tool.

So before we open any box or package on Shabbos, whether by hand or with a tool, we have to find out if the halachah permits it.

Many questions arise regarding opening packages, and there are many opinions, too.

And now let's get to work! If we don't start now we won't be finished till next Shabbos!

Makkeh Bepatish

Playing Music

I didn't know you know how to play music!

This is an electronic keyboard.

That's why you've never seen it!

I've never seen this instrument! What is it called?

Let me guess what your scroll says. We're not allowed to play a keyboard on Shabbos, just like we cannot use any other electronic device!

You're right, but that's not what it says here. Listen patiently!

Do you have other instruments that I am familiar with? I mean, the kind you blow, or pluck on strings, or that you bang on them.

I have a few. They are not professional, but we can make music with them!

No one has ever seen or heard music like that!

Just about.

The instruments we had in the Midbar were not electric, but still we may not play them on Shabbos.

Chazal made a *gezeirah* forbidding playing music on Shabbos, because someone might notice that he needs to repair part of his instrument, and that is *makkeh bepatish*.[260]

Tools Made for Making Noise

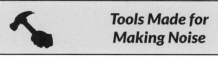

Where did this bell come from? I thought you use only electric bells – This is the kind we used in the desert!

I found it under the bed.

A bell is used to make sound.

Do you have other things that make sounds?

Sure, all those instruments we played before!

Instruments are made to produce music, but I'm asking about things that make sounds that are not music!

I have a whistle!

Although my little brothers think that its purpose is to make people deaf, its real purpose is to make a signal with noise.

This is left over from Purim, a *gragger*!

We actually have all kinds of toys whose function is to make noise:

Now it's my turn to talk. It is forbidden on Shabbos to use anything that is used for making noise.[261]

This clacker,

And a rattle.

This drum

The –

Even though these are not musical instruments, it is forbidden so that people will not repair musical instruments.[261]

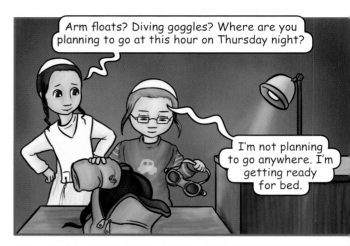

Hamotzi Meirshus Lirshus
Carrying from one place to another

What Is this Melachah, and How Was It Used in Building the Mishkan

Betzalel!

Yes?

I forgot my bus card!

Can you bring it to me? Or throw it out the window?

I'm too tired! Come inside and get it!

Oh, come on! How hard can it be to take a few steps outside and bring me the card?

You're right. I was just being lazy. Here's your bus card.

But I want you to know: Bringing something outside is really a melachah!

When Bnei Yisrael brought donations for the Mishkan from their homes, the act of bringing was called a melachah. The Torah says: ... "The people should do no more melachah... so the people stopped bringing."

So it's forbidden to carry things from place to place on Shabbos.

...es that mean I can't bring water from the kitchen to the dining room?

A siddur from home to shul?

I'll have to explain the details, but this is the melachah of motzi meirshus lirshus.

A person's home is reshus hayachid, while the Mishkan was a reshus harabbim, a public place. The melachah is to bring something from a reshus hayachad to a reshus harabbim, or vice versa.[265]

Reshus Hayachid

You told me we're not allowed to take something out from a reshus hayachid to a reshus harabbim on Shabbos.

But I don't know what a reshus hayachid is!

Actually, I do! My drawer is my private space, my reshus hayachid. No one else may open it.

But I don't really know what a reshus hayachid is!

Wait! Does this mean that on Shabbos I am not allowed to take things from my drawer out to the room, since it belongs to the whole family?

You really do not know what a reshus hayachid is!

A reshus hayachid is a place that is at least four tefachim square and at least 10 tefachim high.[266]

Every house, apartment, or building is a reshus hayachid.

And my drawer?

Your drawer is very important and private drawer inside the house, which is a reshus hayachid.

Therefore, you can always take things out of your drawer or put things into it on Shabbos.

It is permitted to carry things from one room to another, or in and out of a cabinet, as long as they remain in the same reshus hayachid.

95

Hamotzi Meirshus Lirshus

Hamotzi Meirshus Lirshus

Hamotzi Meirshus Lirshus

Carrying from One Reshus Hayachid to Another

Are you working on your scroll again? This one looks different, though!

What are you drawing? A map? A blueprint?

I wanted to describe how cities were built long ago, and I don't think I could describe it with words, so I decided to sketch a picture for you.

The houses stood side by side framing an empty space in the center..

Between the courtyards there were side streets that are called *mevo'os*.

The courtyard was enclosed by a fence.

 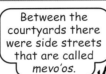

A city was a collection of these *chatzeiros* and *mevo'os*.

I bet a *chatzeir* is a *reshus hayachid*! It is surrounded by a high fence!

Sure. It's a *reshus hayachid*, and the Torah permits carrying things in it on Shabbos.

But Chazal made a *takanah* that it is forbidden to carry things from one person's *reshus hayachid* to another person's *reshus hayachid*.[278]

If that's so, even if a city is surrounded by *eiruv* poles, that's not enough to make it permissible to carry..

Therefore, even if the people living in one *chatzeir* were on the friendliest terms, they would not be allowed to carry objects from one house to another.

It became a *reshus hayachid*, but we are not allowed to carry from one *reshus hayachid* to another *reshus hayachid*.

Eiruvei Chatzeros and Shitufei Mevo'os

So today, explain to me how an *eiruv chatzeiros* works.

Sure. All the owners of the houses within the *chatzeir* make a *kinyan* to become part-owners of some food like a challah. The challah becomes their common property.[279]

Once they do this, it is like they all own the house with the challah, and all the houses are now considered one *reshus hayachid*. Now they can carry anywhere in the *chatzeir*.

So what is *shitufei mevo'os*?

If the city is surrounded by a wall, then all the people in the city could become partners in some food, and that turns the entire city into a single *reshus hayachid*. This enables them to carry in the streets as well.[280]

Eiruv chatzeros
Shitufei mevo'os

Since the food belongs to all the residents of the city, they may carry in all the *mevo'os* as well, or actually in the whole city.

But not all cities are surrounded by a wall! The cities that I know of are surrounded by *eiruv* poles!

If a city is surrounded by a physical wall – then all the Poskim agree that it is permissible to carry in it by making a *shitufei mevo'os*.[281]

If the city is surrounded by *eiruv* poles – each person should find out what opinion his family follows.[282]

Many people carry things outside on Shabbos, and many people do not.

Carrying Where There Is No Eiruv

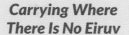

Now just let me ask one last question:

In places where it is forbidden to carry on Shabbos, are there things that I'm allowed to take?

What can I take outside my house?

Well, first of all, you are allowed to wear any kind of clothes, as long as you wear them the regular way.[283]

You can wear a coat, a hat, and all that.

What about glasses? They are not clothes!

You are allowed to wear glasses that you need to see far away, like yours, when leaving the house. We don't suspect that you would take them off and carry them, since you need to wear them all the time to see!

It is forbidden to go outside wearing reading glasses, since we suspect that the person might take them off outside and carry them in a *reshus harabbim*.[284]

What if I want to carry my baby brother outside to a place with no *eiruv*?

It is forbidden to hold a baby in your arms or in a stroller and take him from one *reshus* to another. If he is able to walk by himself, you can take him for a walk with you.

There are other items that you might be allowed to carry, such as jewelry, but you must ask about each one.[285]

Conclusion

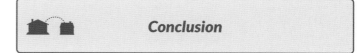

What is all this, Betzalel? What are all these packages?

Are you moving?

I'm going back to my real home! To the Midbar!

But why? Don't you like it here?

I enjoyed having you with me every single day! I learned so much!

Zorei'a and *choreish* and *kotzeir*, *me'ameir*, *dosh*, *zoreh*, *boreir*, *merakeid* and –

That's exactly why.

We've finished learning the *melachah* of carrying from one *reshus* to another. That is the last of the 39 *melachos*.

I am packing up my last pictures and now I'm going to leave!

Betzalel wait! You forgot to take the scrolls!

I'm leaving them for you, so you can review the halachos again and again!

Goodbye Betzalel! I'll never forget you! I'm going to miss you every day!

I'm not abandoning you altogether. I plan to send you someone to take my place.

Wait patiently! The surprise will come soon!

Sources

Introduction

1 *Shabbos 49b; Rashi, ibid.*

Definitions

2 *Beitzah 32b, gezeirah because of a permanent tent; see Shulchan Aruch, 315:1. The details of the halachos of ohel are clarified later on in the melachah of Boneh, Hilchos Ohel.*

3 *Shabbos 96b*

4 *Shabbos, Chapter 12, Mishnah 5; Shulchan Aruch, 340:4*

5 *Shulchan Aruch, 308:3*

6 *Rambam, Hilchos Shabbos, 24:13 (see other reasons there)*

Zorei'a

7 *According to Rambam, Hilchos Shabbos 8:2*

8 *When grafting, care must be taken to avoid kilayim*

9 *Rambam, Hilchos Shabbos, 8:2*

10 *Shulchan Aruch, 336:3*

11 *In this case, where his clothes got wet, there might be an issur of melabein.*

12 *Yerushalmi, Shabbos 7:2*

13 *In Gemara Moed Katan 2b, there is a debate about why someone who weeds or who waters plants is chayav. According to Rabbah, these acts are included in the melachah of choreish because plowing is done to soften the ground, and this is also accomplished by watering and weeding. According to Rav Yosef, these actions are included in the melachah of zorei'a because watering and weeding help the plant grow, and that is the melachah of zorei'a: helping plants grow in the ground. The Rambam rules that weeding is a toladah of choreish and watering is a toladah of zorei'a. But the Rokeach, the Smag and the Hagahos Maimoniyos are of the opinion that watering makes him chayav for two melachos, meaning that he transgressed two issurim with one act. That is what the Mishnah Berurah wrote in 336:26, but the Shaar Hatziyun 18 writes that it is possible to differentiate as follows: if the land has been sown, then he is guilty of them both, but if it has not been sown, but is ready to be plowed, then he is guilty only of choreish.*

Choreish

14 *Rambam, Hilchos Shabbos 8:1*

15 *Shabbos 73b*

16 *Shabbos 73b; Rambam Hilchos Shabbos, 21:2*

17 *Rambam, ibid. 3; Shulchan Aruch, 337:2. It should be noted regarding a tiled floor, that according to the Mechaber, ibid., it is permitted to sweep a tiled or paved floor. He also brings an opinion that permits it on ground that is not tiled or paved, but the Rema holds that it is forbidden because of the unpaved floor. But in any case, he writes there in Biur Halachah that if most of the homes in the city are tiled then it is permitted, and based on this it is evident that there is no prohibition of sweeping the floor in our day.*

18 *Shulchan Aruch, 338:5*

Kotzeir

19 *Shulchan Aruch, 336:12*

20 *Shabbos 73b; Rambam, Hilchos Shabbos, 8:3*

21 *Shevisas Hashabbos, Meleches Kotzeir 2*

22 *Beitzah 5:2*

23 *Shulchan Aruch, 336:1*

24 *Shulchan Aruch, 336:13*

25 *Shulchan Aruch, 305:18*

26 *Mishnah Berurah, 305:1*

27 *Shulchan Aruch, 336:10*

Me'ameir

28 *See Shabbos 7:2, in Peirush Hamishnayos Leharambam and in Rabbeinu Ovadiah Bartenura, ibid.; see Eglei Tal, Meleches Me'ameir, 1.*

29 *Shulchan Aruch, 340:10; see Mishnah Berurah 340:38*

30 *Rambam, 21:11*

31 *Shulchan Aruch, 340:9*

32 *Shulchan Aruch, 335:5*

33 *Shulchan Aruch, 335:5*

34 *Mishnah Berurah 335:17*

Dosh

35 *Me'iri, Shabbos 73b*

36 *Rambam, Hilchos Shabbos, 8:10*

37 *See Shulchan Aruch, 320:1; Mishnah Berurah, 320:5*

38 *Shulchan Aruch, 319:6; Mishnah Berurah, 319:21*

39 *Shabbos 95a; Rambam, Hilchos Shabbos, 8:7; According to the Yerushalmi (Shabbos 7:2) he is chayav because of kotzeir.*

40 *Shulchan Aruch, 320:9*

41 *Mishnah Berurah, 320:33, and the source is Ra"n (Shabbos 51b). And Rashi writes the reason — because he generates the water on Shabbos.*

42 *Shulchan Aruch, 320:1*

Zoreh

43 *Rambam, Hilchos Shabbos, 8:11*

44 *Shu"t Rabi Akiva Eiger 20; see Biur Halachah, 319, beginning with 'mefazer'*

45 *Eglei Tal, Meleches Zoreh, 5*

Boreir

46 *Rambam, Hilchos Shabbos, 8:12-13; see Biur Halachah, 319, beginning with le'echol miyad*

47 *Mishnah Berurah, Introduction to 319; see Shulchan Aruch, 319:4*

48 *Mishnah Berurah, Introduction to 319; see Shulchan Aruch, 319:1*

49 *Mishnah Berurah, Introduction to 319; see Shulchan Aruch, 319:2*

50 *Shabbos 74a; Tosafos ibid., beginning with 'hayu'*

51 *Aruch Hashulchan, 319:9; and see Shemiras Shabbos K'Hilchasah, 3:3*

52 *Biur Halachah, 319, beginning with 'hayu'; and see there that the Pri Megadim questions this.*

53 *Shulchan Aruch, 319:8; see Shemiras Shabbos K'Hilchasah, 3:21*

54 *Shulchan Aruch, 321:9; see Shemiras Shabbos K'Hilchasah, ibid.*

Tochein

55 *Rambam, Hilchos Shabbos, 8:15*

56 *Rambam, Hilchos Shabbos, 8:15*

57 *Shulchan Aruch, 321:12; the Rema permits eating it immediately, and the Mishnah Berurah brings opinions stating that it is forbidden even immediately.*

58 *Shulchan Aruch, 321:9*

59 *Shulchan Aruch, 321:10, and the reason is because of uvda d'chol, it is a weekday activity; Mishnah Berurah, ibid. 36.*

Merakeid

60 *Rabbeinu Ovadiah Mibartenura; Peirush Hamishnayos Larambam in Mishnayos Shabbos, 7:2*

Losh

61 *Shabbos 49b; and in Rashi ibid.*

62 *Rambam, Hilchos Shabbos, 8:16; Shulchan Aruch, 321:14; Chazon Ish, 59:8*

63 *Mishnah Berurah, 321:66*

64 *Shulchan Aruch, 321:16*

65 *Mishnah Berurah, 321:57*

66 *Shulchan Aruch, 324:3; see Biur Halachah ibid. beginning with 'uma'avir'; see 321:14, in the Mechaber, where he writes only one shinui.*

67 *Shulchan Aruch, 321:16; Mishnah Berurah, ibid. 63*

68 *Shabbos 18a; see Mishnah Berurah, 321:50; that there are Rishonim who ruled the opposite: If he kneaded a dough, then the issur is only mid'Rabbanan.*

Bishul

Sources

69 *Rambam Hilchos Shabbos 9:1-6; Mishnah Berurah 318:1*

70 *According to Pri Migadim, 318:47:7; Harav Shlomo Zalman Auerbach in Shemiras Shabbos K'Hilchasah concurs 1:61; and Harav Yosef Shalom Elyashiv in sefer Me'or Hashabbos Vol. II 8:2*

71 *Rambam, Hilchos Shabbos, 9:1; Eglei Tal, Meleches Ofeh 1; and it brings there that the Yerushalmi holds that baking, frying and roasting are a toladah of bishul.*

72 *Maseches Shabbos, 39a; Shulchan Aruch, 318:3*

73 *Maseches Shabbos, 39a; Shulchan Aruch, 318:3; and the reason is because people don't interchange sun and fire, but the toldos ohr and toldos chamah can be interchanged.*

74 *Maseches Shabbos 40b*

75 *There are opinions in the poskim that this shiur is more serious, and that one who cooks in a kli sheini in any way, according to all opinions; cited in Mishnah Berurah 318:48.*

76 *Shulchan Aruch 318:9*

77 *Magen Avraham 318:28 citing the Yerushalmi, that they distanced the kli rishon even when it is not yet yad soledes bo.*

78 *Tosafos Shabbos 42:2 beginning with 'aval'*

79 *Shulchan Aruch, 318:10*

80 *Magen Avraham, 318:35, that the lower one overpowers the upper one and cools it.*

81 *Mishnah Berurah 318:82; see Biur Halachah, ibid., beginning with 'vehu' which brings that there are those who differ and are more lenient about this.*

82 *Shabbos 42b; Shulchan Aruch, 318:5; Mishnah Berurah, 42*

83 *Shulchan Aruch, 318: 5; Magen Avraham 18*

84 *Shulchan Aruch, 318:13; Shaar Hatziyun, 68; and the Shulchan Aruch Harav, 14, is also lenient about other liquids.*

85 *Shulchan Aruch, 318:4*

86 *See Shu"t Mekor Chaim, Orach Chaim, 7; Aruch Hashulchan, 318:28; Shu"t Igros Moshe, Vol. IV, 74:15 and others. Although*

there are those who permit it.

87 *Magen Avraham, 318:45; Mishnah Berurah, ibid. 65*

88 *Shulchan Aruch, 318:4; regarding the bones in the chicken, the poskim discuss if they need to be soft and edible in order to consider the dish as being cooked and thus to allow bishul achar bishul. It is known that Harav Shlomo Zalman Auerbach was strict about this in Shu"t Minchas Shlomo 6; however, Shevet Halevi 3:93 permits it; the Chut Shani differentiates if it is something commonly eaten or not.*

89 *Shulchan Aruch, 318:4; see Biur Halachah, ibid., beginning with 'yesh bo'; that according to the Rambam and the Rashba, then with a moist thing as well, there is no bishul achar bishul.*

90 *If it cooled down – then there is bishul achar bishul according to all opinions; if it is still hot – then the Mechaber says it is forbidden, and the Rema permits it.*

91 *Shulchan Aruch, 318:5*

92 *The Rema takes the stricter view; the Shulchan Aruch brings both opinions but does not rule; from the Magen Avraham, 19, it is evident that he understands from the Shulchan Aruch that it was lenient; Harav Ovadiah Yosef ruled in Yabia Omer, Vol. VI, 48, like those who are lenient, but the Kaf Hachaim and the Kitzur Shulchan Aruch written by Harav Toledano take the stricter view; and in a kli shelishi it is permitted but there are those who are strict according to the Yere'im.*

Shehiyah

93 *Shulchan Aruch, 253:1*

94 *Shulchan Aruch, 253:1; and in Biur Halachah, ibid., beginning with 'ela', in the name of Rabi Akiva Eiger. Some say that this is also only permitted when it is cooked to a ma'achal ben drusa'i from Erev Shabbos. Shulchan Aruch Harav, ibid. 1; some say that it is permitted in any case.*

95 *Shemiras Shabbos K'Hilchasah 1:71 in the name of Harav Shlomo Zalman Auerbach*

Sources

Chazarah

96 *Shulchan Aruch, 253:2*

97 *Shulchan Aruch and Rema, 253:2; but when one of the conditions is absent, it is forbidden, because it appears like bishul; Mishnah Berurah, ibid. 55 and 61: When it is not completely cooked there is an issur d'oraisa involved.*

Hatmanah

98 *Shulchan Aruch, 257:1; Mishnah Berurah, ibid. 1*

99 *Shulchan Aruch, 257:1; Mishnah Berurah, ibid. 1*

100 *Shulchan Aruch, 257:6; and in Mishnah Berurah, 258:2 – that it cannot be wrapped in something that heats it.*

101 *Shulchan Aruch, 257:4*

102 *Shulchan Aruch, 257:5, that when he transfers it he cools it a bit and indicates that he is not particular about the heat, and therefore, there is no concern that he will come to boil it up.*

103 *Shemiras Shabbos K'Hilchasah, 1:72*

104 *Shulchan Aruch, 257:1, for fear that he will come to wrap it in ash that has embers and he will come to rake the coals.*

Gozeiz

105 *Rambam, Hilchos Shabbos 9:7-8*

106 *See Shulchan Aruch, 340:1; Mishnah Berurah, ibid. 2*

107 *See Shulchan Aruch, 340:1; Mishnah Berurah, ibid. 2*

108 *ibid.*

109 *Shulchan Aruch, 303:27; Mishnah Berurah, ibid. 86; although a brush, where it is not psik reisha that it pulls out hair, is permitted for use.*

Melabein

110 *Shabbos 142:2; Rashi beginning with 'mekancho'*

111 *Shemiras Shabbos K'Hilchasah 12:40; based on Shulchan Aruch, 302:6*

112 *Rema 302:1; Mishnah Berurah, ibid. 7*

113 *Rambam, Hilchos Shabbos, 9:11: "sechitah (wringing) is one of the necessities of laundering."*

114 *Shulchan Aruch, 301:45*

115 *Mishnah Berurah, 301: 170; Shaar Hatziyun, 212*

Menapeitz

116 *Shabbos 73a; see Rashi and Me'iri, ibid., and see Mishnah Berurah, end of 344*

Tzovea

117 *Mishnah Berurah, 327:12*

118 *Mishnah Berurah, 320:56*

119 *Shulchan Aruch, 320:19*

120 *Shaar Hatziyun, 318:65; Shemiras Shabbos K'Hilchasah, 11:38*

Toveh

121 *Mishnah Berurah, end of 344*

Oseh **Shtei Batei Nirin**

122 *See Tosafos Yom Tov and Tiferes Yisrael, Shabbos 17:2; Tosafos Ri"d 214, Shabbos 73a*

Oreig

123 *Rambam, Hilchos Shabbos, 9:19*

Potzei'a

124 *Rambam, Hilchos Shabbos, 9:20; see additional commentaries in the Raavad, ibid.; Tosafos Ri"d, Shabbos 73a; Ran, ibid.*

Kosheir

125 *Shulchan Aruch, 317:1*

126 *Shabbos, 74a*

127 *Rema 317:1; Mishnah Berurah, introduction, ibid.; Shulchan Aruch Harav, ibid. 1*

128 *Mishnah Berurah and Shulchan Aruch Harav, ibid.*

Sources

129 *Mishnah Berurah, ibid.; notes that that some say that a knot that is opened within seven days is not a kesher shel kayama.*

130 *Rema 317:1*

131 *Rema, ibid.*

132 *Rema, ibid.; Mishnah Berurah, ibid. 15; see Biur Halachah, ibid., beginning with 'dino.'*

133 *This type of knot is permitted, as the Rema rules, 317:5*

134 *Mishnah Berurah, 317:29*

135 *Shulchan Aruch Harav, 317:3; but there are those who differ and forbid it to be tied for more than 24 hours; see Avnei Nezer*

136 *Shulchan Aruch, 317:5*

137 *Rema 317:2; see there that the issur is only in an act that has exertion, but the Mishnah Berurah, ibid. 20, cites the opinion of the poskim that even when there is no exertion, tirchah, it is forbidden.*

138 *Shemiras Shabbos K'Hilchasah, 16:59, in the name of Harav Shlomo Zalman Auerbach; Chut Shani, Vol. II, 34:13 p. 232*

139 *Ketzos Hashulchan in Badei Hashulchan, 123:4*

Matir

140 *Rema 317:1; Mishnah Berurah, ibid. 7*

Tofeir

141 *Shulchan Aruch, 340:6; Mishnah Berurah, ibid. 27; Shaar Hatzion 60*

142 *Mishnah Berurah, ibid.*

143 *Shemiras Shabbos K'Hilchasah 28:5, and comment 17*

144 *Shulchan Aruch, 340:14*

145 *Shemiras Shabbos K'Hilchasah 15:74*

146 *Shulchan Aruch, 340:6*

147 *Shulchan Aruch ibid.; Shemiras Shabbos K'Hilchasah 15:67*

Korei'a

148 *Shabbos 75a*

149 *Rambam, Hilchos Shabbos, 10:10-11*

150 *Mishnah Berurah, 340:45; according to Shulchan Aruch, 314:10*

151 *In the place of the letters it is forbidden because of mocheik*

Tzad

152 *See Rambam, 10:19*

153 *Rambam 10:19; Mishnah Berurah, 316:4*

154 *Shulchan Aruch 316:3; and even though poeple often catch them so that they should not be bothersome they are considered "ein bemino nitzad" and it is forbidden only mid'Rabbanan.*

155 *Shulchan Aruch, ibid.*

156 *Mishnah Berurah, 316:18; and the reason that it is not forbidden from the Torah is because the animal might not get caught in the trap.*

157 *Rema 316:12; Mishnah Berurah, ibid. 59*

158 *Mishnah Berurah, 316:54*

159 *Rema, 316:12*

160 *Shulchan Aruch, 316:7; Mishnah Berurah, ibid. 27*

161 *Shulchan Aruch, 316:10*

Shocheit

162 *Rambam, Hilchos Shabbos 11:1*

163 *Mishnah Berurah, 316:30; in this way it is spoiled.*

164 *Shulchan Aruch Harav, 316:14*

165 *Shemiras Shabbos K'Hilchasah, 25:5; note 28*

166 *Based on Shulchan Aruch, 252:1*

Mafshit

167 *Mishnas Hashabbos, 31*

Me'abeid

168 *Rambam, 11:5-6; and in chapter 23:10; Mishnah Berurah, 227:12*

Sources

169 *Yoreh Deah, 69*

170 *Mishnah Berurah, 321:21*

171 *Shabbos 108b; and in Rashi, ibid., that the reason is because of me'abed; and the Rambam in Hilchos Shabbos 22:10, wrote that it is forbidden because of pickling, which looks like bishul.*

172 *Mishnah Berurah, 321:14; Ketzos Hashulchan, 128:3*

Memacheik

173 *Rambam Hilchos Shabbos, 11:5*

174 *Shulchan Aruch, 323:9; and the prohibition is not only with cream, but also with a special wipe used for this; Shemiras Shabbos K'Hilchasah 12:24*

175 *Rambam, Hilchos Shabbos, 11:6*

176 *Shulchan Aruch, 328:25; Mishnah Berurah, ibid. 81*

177 *Shulchan Aruch, 328:17 and 25*

178 *Rema, 321:19*

179 *Rema, ibid.; Biur Halachah, ibid., beginning with 'bema'achal'*

Mesarteit

180 *Rambam, Hilchos Shabbos, 11:17*

181 *Rashi, Shabbos 75b*

182 *Shemiras Shabbos K'Hilchasah 11:15*

Mechateich

183 *Rambam, Hilchos Shabbos, 11:7; and see Mishnah Berurah, 322:18*

184 *Rambam, ibid.*

185 *Shulchan Aruch, 340:13; see there Mishnah Berurah and Biur Halachah*

186 *Mishnah Berurah, 322:12*

187 *Shulchan Aruch, 321:12; and see Shu"t Igros Moshe 4:74, Meleches Tochein, 3, in the definition of 'dak dak'*

Koseiv

188 *Shabbos 103a*

189 *Rambam, Hilchos Shabbos, 11:15*

190 *Rambam ibid.; see Mishnah Berurah, 340:22*

191 *Shulchan Aruch, 340:4*

192 *Rambam, Hilchos Shabbos, 11:14; and see Mishnah Berurah, 340:22:7*

193 *Rambam, ibid.; Mishnah Berurah, ibid.*

194 *Mishnah Berurah, 340:22:3; there it is clarified that if he does not add to it, and only renews a bit – then he is exempt; but if he writes ink on a lighter red ink, then he is guilty of both mocheik and koseiv.*

195 *Rambam, Hilchos Shabbos, 11:17*

196 *Rambam, Hilchos Shabbos, 23:12; Rashi Bei-tzah 37a; says another reason is because 'mimtzo cheftzecha' that one should not engage in weekday matters; but one is permitted to buy for Shabbos, if he doesn't mention the term 'purchase', rather refers to it as 'giving'. Likewise, they should not discuss a price or measurement.*

197 *Rambam, Hilchos Shabbos, 23:12; see another reason in the next comment*

198 *Shulchan Aruch, 306:7; and see Mishnah Berurah, ibid. 34; that elsewhere Chazal did not permit shevus in the place of a mitzvah, and only here, because the issur is only due to uvda d'chol, it is permitted in the place of a mitzvah.*

Mocheik

199 *Rambam, Hilchos Shabbos, 11:9*

200 *Magen Avraham, 519:4; Mishnah Berurah, ibid. 11*

201 *Mishnah Berurah, 340:41*

202 *Rema, 340:3*

203 *Mishnah Berurah, 340:15*

204 *Badei Hashulchan 144:3; and can be derived from the lack of mention by the Shulchan Aruch Harav, 340:4*

Boneh

205 *Rambam, Hilchos Shabbos, 10:12*

206 *Shulchan Aruch Harav, 314:2*

207 *Shemiras Shabbos K'Hilchasah, 23:39*

208 *Shemiras Shabbos K'Hilchahah, 20:43*

Sources

209 *Rema, 314:1*

210 *Tosafos Maseches Shabbos, 102b; Shulchan Aruch, 313:6, 9; see Taz, ibid. 6 that the issur is because of makkeh bepatish*

211 *Magen Avraham, 313:12; Mishnah Berurah, ibid. 45*

212 *Rambam, Hilchos Shabbos, 10:13; see Shulchan Aruch, 313:9*

213 *Shulchan Aruch, 315:1; Mishnah Berurah, ibid. 2*

214 *Shulchan Aruch, 315:2; Mishnah Berurah, ibid. 2*

214 *Shulchan Aruch, 315:2, but according to the Rif and Rabbeinu Chananel it seems forbidden even to add to an existing tent, because an ohel that is the width of a tefach is a d'Oraisa.*

215 *Shulchan Aruch, 315:1; it is a gezeirah because of a permanent ohel (Mishnah Berurah ibid. 1)*

216 *Shu"t Noda B'Yehudah (Tinyana Orach Chaim 30); and the Chazon Ish, 52:6, cites as another reason for the prohibition uvda d'chol, weekday-like work.*

217 *Shulchan Aruch, 315:5; and see Biur Halachah, ibid., beginning with 'lechatchilah'*

218 *Shulchan Aruch, 315:1; that the main part of the ohel is the roof that covers all of it, and therefore it is ruled as a gezeirah because of an ohel keva. However, a temporary partition is not considered an ohel at all (Mishnah Berurah ibid. 3)*

219 *Shulchan Aruch, 315:1; Mishnah Berurah, ibid. 6; and in Shaar Hatziyun*

220 *Shulchan Aruch, 315:1; because it is considered a mechitzah with regard to a sukkah and as such, it is considered building (Mishnah Berurah, ibid. 4)*

Soseir

221 *Like any act of destruction on Shabbos, which is not punishable but is forbidden mid'Rabbanan; Shabbos 106a; Tosafos, ibid., beginning with 'chutz'*

222 *According to Shabbos 122b*

223 *See Shulchan Aruch, 303:26; Mishnah Berurah, ibid. 83*

Mechabeh

224 *Rambam, Hilchos Shabbos, 12:2*

225 *Shulchan Aruch, 277:1*

226 *Mishnah Berurah, ibid. 3*

227 *Mishnah Berurah, 277:2*

228 *Shulchan Aruch, 334:26*

229 *Shulchan Aruch, ibid.*

230 *Shulchan Aruch, 334:22*

231 *See Shulchan Aruch, 334:24, citing a dispute in the poskim if causing a fire to go out is also permitted in this way of pouring water around the fire, and he rules that one can be lenient.*

232 *Shulchan Aruch, 334:1; and see 11, where some say that it is permitted to save anything into courtyard that has an eiruv.*

233 *Shulchan Aruch, ibid.*

234 *Shulchan Aruch, 334:8; because he is taking it out by wearing it, we do not suspect that he will put out the fire (Mishnah Berurah, ibid. 18)*

235 *Shulchan Aruch, 334:12*

Mav'ir

236 *Rambam, 12:1; and in Orchos Shabbos16:3*

237 *Shulchan Aruch, 277:2*

238 *Magen Avraham, 514:9*

239 *See Shulchan Aruch, ibid., that it is forbidden only when the fire is a bit close to the door.*

240 *Shabbos 12a; Shulchan Aruch, 275:1*

241 *Shulchan Aruch, 275:2*

242 *Shulchan Aruch, 275:3*

243 *Mishnah Berurah, 275:4; and the Mechaber's opinion is to forbid it even with paraffin candles, but the Mishnah Berurah rules that with our candles we need not suspect that anyone will adjust the wick, and they are therefore permitted.*

244 *Even when there are various levels of intensity of the light; Shemiras Shabbos K'Hilchasah 13:32, in the name of Rav Shlomo Zalman Auerbach.*

245 *Shu"t Minchas Shlomo, 1:12*

246 *Some say that it is because of nolad,*

that by activating it, a new electric current is created in the wires (Minchas Shlomo 9); some say it is because of boneh, as it forms a new functional unit (Chazon Ish, Orach Chaim 50:9)

247 *Shulchan Aruch, 326:1; and the prohibition is even when it is not yad soledes hahem; Tehillah L'Dovid, ibid. 3*

248 *Shulchan Aruch, 326:1*

Makkeh Bepatish

249 *Rambam, Hilchos Shabbos, 10:16*

250 *Shulchan Aruch, 302:1*

251 *Shulchan Aruch, 509:1; Mishnah Berurah, ibid. 1; Shemiras Shabbos K'Hilchasah, 15:77*

252 *Shulchan Aruch, 339:4*

253 *Shulchan Aruch, 323:7; and see there that there is another hour that makes it more lenient, and one of the reasons is because bedieved, the food is not forbidden because of this (Biur Halachah, ibid., beginning with 'mutar')*

254 *Shulchan Aruch, 302:3*

255 *Shemiras Shabbos K'Hilchasah, 15:46*

256 *Mishnah Berurah, 317:18*

257 *Ketzos Hashulchan, 146:3*

258 *Rema, 317:2; Mishnah Berurah, ibid. 20*

259 *Biur Halachah, 318, beginning with 'vehadachasan'; and see there that the Pri Megadim is strict about this*

260 *Shulchan Aruch, 338:1*

261 *Rema, 338:1*

262 *Shulchan Aruch, 339:3; Mishnah Berurah, ibid. 9*

263 *Shulchan Aruch, 339:2*

264 *Magen Avraham, 326:8; Shulchan Aruch Harav, 339:6; because of the possible issur of sechitah, wringing*

Hamotzi Meirshus Lirshus

265 *Shabbos 96b*

266 *Shulchan Aruch, 345:2*

267 *Shulchan Aruch, 345:7*

268 *Shulchan Aruch, 346:1*

269 *Shulchan Aruch, 345:14*

270 *Shulchan Aruch, 346:1-2*

271 *Shulchan Aruch, 345:19; and see there regarding a pillar between 9 and 10 tefachim high*

272 *Shulchan Aruch, 346:1*

273 *Shulchan Aruch, 345:12*

274 *Shulchan Aruch, ibid. 18*

275 *Shulchan Aruch, ibid. 5*

276 *Shulchan Aruch, 364:2*

277 *Shulchan Aruch 362:11*

278 *Rambam Hilchos Eiruvin, 1:2*

279 *Rambam Hilchos Eiruvin 1:4-6*

280 *Rambam, ibid.*

281 *Shulchan Aruch, 364:2*

282 *See Biur Halachah 345 beginning with 'she'ein'; Mishnah Berurah, ibid. 23 and others.*

283 *Shulchan Aruch, 301:14*

284 *Shemiras Shabbos K'Hilchasah, 18:16*

285 *See Shulchan Aruch, 303:18; and Biur Halachah, ibid.*

There are 39 avos melachos.

(Shabbos 73a)

  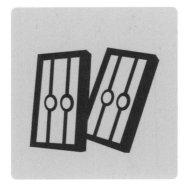